New Plants from Old

To Jean Hobbins and her foraged garden;

to my grandfather Alfred Theophilous Edwards and his

wife Jan, who taught me that gardens need not be bought.

New Plants from Old

simple, natural, no-cost
PLANT PROPAGATION

JACKIE FRENCH

AIRD BOOKS
Melbourne

This edition first published in 2007 by Aird Books,
an imprint of Manna Trading Pty Ltd
PO Box 122
Flemington, Vic. 3031
Phone (03) 9376 4461

First edition published by Aird Books in 1991,
reprinted 1993

National Library of Australia
Cataloguing-in-publication data

French, Jackie.
    New plants from old : simple, natural, no-cost
    plant propagation.

    Completely rev. and updated 2nd ed.
    Includes index.
    ISBN 9780947214562 (pbk.).

    1. Plant propagation. 2. Gardening - Australia.
    3. Gardening - New Zealand. I. Title.

631.530994

Text and cover design and layout by
Pauline Deakin, Captured Concepts
Text illustrations by Greg Jorgenson

Contents

Preface

You don't have to pay money to have a garden.

Money helps, of course — one of my great joys is mooching around a nursery. But the plants in my garden that I love most are the ones that have been given to me, as cuttings or seeds. They're the ones that give me memories, as well as flowers or fruit.

The red geranium from Jean's garden; the floppy Duchesse de Brabant rose from Natalie; the vast chilacayote vine with its tons of fruit that grew from a seed a reader sent me, when I complained that my chilacayotes were bitter. The backbone of my garden has been grown from seeds or cuttings, and every time I mooch around it my garden gives me stories too.

Gardens don't HAVE to be bought. They can be collected, with love and happiness, as they have been for thousands of years.

But having a cheap — or even free — garden isn't the only reason for learning how to propagate plants. Taking cuttings and collecting seeds also helps to preserve the hundreds of species that would otherwise vanish every year.

Earth is the sum of its living species — insect, plant and animal. And every day there are fewer and fewer, as more species are wiped out. Even the number of plant species that are 'useful' to humans is getting smaller because patented seeds are more profitable to sell; because we choose to eat only the limited recognisable varieties that grow well with artificial fertilisers and pesticides; and because that small square of the environment we are closest to, our back garden, is becoming as commercial as any other aspect of our lives, dependent on large companies for its plants and beauty.

NEVER think that growing your own plants is complicated. It isn't. The detailed suggestions given in this book about seed and potting mixtures, best times to collect seed and take cuttings, planting techniques, and so on will help give the best results. But many gardeners grow glorious gardens just with seeds stuffed in uncleaned glass jars for sowing in the next year;

cuttings are bunged into any pot around with whatever happens to be in it; bits of shrub are stuck into water to root.

As long as you have a basic idea of what to do you'll probably succeed. Plants have seeded, flowered, and seeded for millennia without us. Humans really need have only a small role in the world of plants. When in doubt, just bung it in. It'll probably grow.

These days our entertainment is controlled by television multinationals. Our clothes are designed overseas and made in factories. But there's no reason why our gardens have to be controlled by large companies. Garden plants, including fruit and vegetables, are everyone's heritage. All we need is a little knowledge and the desire to keep them.

A tale of an old-fashioned garden

I learnt about gardening from an elderly woman called Jean. She lived next door (though next door was a kilometre away down the valley).

Jean had green fingers and carried a large handbag. The handbag was usually slightly grubby and filled with plastic bags – just in case, she said, she found a plant from which to take a cutting. She usually did. Senior citizens outings, CWA excursions, Christmas parties; anywhere she went she'd find a plant to take a bit of, or a flower that was seeding.

Jean had a classic cottage garden – the sort that grows from seeds and cuttings, not from garden centres. It has been accumulating for 60 years, the pots and cuttings going with her as she moved from state to state.

Down from the bank were geraniums, red and pink and pale mauve, plain-leafed and variegated, perfumed in half a dozen scents. Some were from her mother's garden, who had got them from her mother, whose father was a sea captain and brought them back in the days before quarantine. (She gave me a piece of one, and I gave a bit to a German student who gave it to his girlfriend; she wrote to me last year to say she'd sent some cuttings to some Danish students she had met in Crete. They're well-travelled geraniums!)

In the front were modern roses; her brother-in-law had brought up some prunings in wet newspaper from Victoria and she struck them in wet sand. There was an old-fashioned rose out the back; she'd come upon that in the bush and stuck a sprig in her pocket. Then there was the grape she'd grown from a seed of the best grape she'd ever tasted; and the wisteria she'd taken as a root cutting from the garden of an old house being pulled down – she thought the colour, a deep purple not seen any more, was too good to waste.

Bulbs were bought at the CWA stall in town, dug from other people's gardens or the roadside and thrown into a pot; plant snippets or seeds were brought back in her handbag. Every plant in the garden had a story, and a host of memories attached. It made those planned gardens I'd known as a child — bought from garden centres on Sunday afternoons, where nothing was exchanged except money — seem sterile and unfriendly.

Jean gave me seeds from her garden, or cuttings brought back from bus trips with the senior citizens — and next time she came up to my place she expected to see them growing. I was always afraid that if they weren't thriving she mightn't feed me any more sponge cake (made of duck eggs with home-grown raspberries, and cream from a cow called Jackie — I was never sure if that was a compliment or not). But, anyhow, I made sure that anything Jean gave me was planted. And just about every time it grew.

Not very long ago nearly all gardens were 'borrowed' like this; only the rich bought their plants. A slip of a new rose might go round a whole town; and seeds were kept for next year.

Although plants have fruited and seeded for millions of years without the aid of nurseries, I recently overheard a major nursery proprietor talk with contempt about 'backyard seed collectors'. Like many other aspects of our lives that we used to control ourselves, gardens are falling into the hands of the experts.

May this book help people go against the 'trend' of buying patented seeds from soulless multinationals, by letting them grow plants with love, friendship, a few twigs, and seeds in an old envelope.

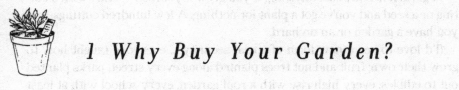

1 Why Buy Your Garden?

Cost

A garden might have 10 fruit trees. At the time of writing these cost between $15 and $25 each — which soon adds up. Vegetable seeds to provide for a family (a lot more if you buy punnets) may total about $100 a year. Add at least 50 or so shrubs you need to decorate your garden at about $10 each, plus climbers, flowers, and maybe a potted cyclamen for the office desk, and you've got a nice gigantic bill.

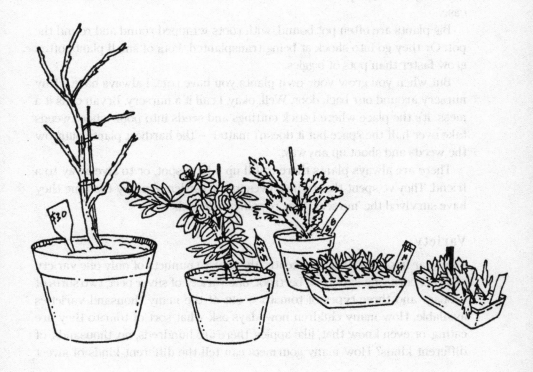

Oh, and don't forget 12 punnets of seedlings for the front garden, and another 12 punnets when those die ...

A garden needn't cost anything if you grow it yourself — start with a cutting or a seed and you've got a plant for nothing. A few hundred cuttings, and you have a garden or an orchard.

(I'd love to see a new form of social security ... everyone taught how to grow their own; fruit and nut trees planted along every street, parks planted out to edibles, every high-rise with a roof garden, every school with at least one fruit tree for every kid enrolled. Replace football with 'dodgeball', as the players dodge around the fruit trees on the oval ...)

Time

I am constantly amazed — even after watching it for more than 30 years — how a seed planted one spring may grow and give fruit long before a three-year-old grafted tree bought from a nursery.

Why?

Less root disturbance; no shock as a tree grown in the moist sub-tropics goes into cold dry ground down here.

Most garden centre customers like BIG plants which they think will give them a great display sooner than a tiny one would. But often this isn't the case.

Big plants are often pot bound, with roots wrapped round and round the pot. Or they go into shock at being transplanted. Pots of small plants often grow faster than pots of biggies.

But when you grow your own plants you have LOTS. I always have a tiny nursery around our back door. Well, okay, I call it a nursery. Bryan calls it a mess. It's the place where I stick cuttings and seeds into pots, where weeds take over half the space but it doesn't matter — the hardiest plants outgrow the weeds and shoot up anyway.

There are always plants there to fill up a bare spot, or to give away to a friend. They've spent their whole lives in my garden. And by the time they have survived the 'nursery' they're going to do well.

Variety

This year in our local garden centre there were punnets of only one variety of sweet corn, one variety of beetroot, one variety of silver beet, two sorts of cabbage and three types of tomato — out of the many thousand varieties available. How many children nowadays ask what sort of tomato they are eating, or even know that, like apples, there are hundreds, no, thousands, of different kinds? How many gourmets can tell the different kinds of sweet corn, or know the seasons for the different onions? How many cooks of frozen anonymous green beans ever dream of the dozens of kinds of beans they could be growing?

This year we grew seven different beans from seed kept from year to year. I'd as soon serve the same sort of beans two nights in a row as I'd serve the same main course. Every year we have apple tastings comparing the flavours of the 125 varieties of apple we grow. (Which is, admittedly, a bit excessive, especially as there are just the two of us at home now. But I am very fond of apples.) This year, friends have offered us deep purple potatoes, black capsicum, white eggplant, beans as long as your arm, and a sweet hardy melon so tough you have to crack the skin with an axe; and we offer our new experiences in exchange.

Don't be limited by what's commercially available. There is no such thing as a single tomato taste, or peach taste, or orange taste, no matter what information the artificial flavour manufacturers give us. There is a whole world of food to be discovered.

The joy of experimenting

This is the age of uniformity — watching the same show as everyone else, wearing the same clothes as everyone else — and it is spreading to our gardens. In last century's catalogues there were literally hundreds of varieties of apples, peaches, plums; page after page of roses; and bulb lists that make our modern catalogues look scrawny. There were probably over a thousand apple varieties compared to perhaps the dozen popularly grown now.

Even these enormous lists still don't give a true idea of the diversity of last century. The orchard where we live was started in the 1890s. I walked round it with the ex-owner a few years before he died, comparing the peach, walnut, and apple trees, all grown from seed, many of which are quite different from any we see in the shops now.

We have been brain-washed to believe that anything that doesn't come 'true-to-type' must be bad — which it is, from a commercial grower's point of view. Customers won't buy a fruit they aren't used to. Modern varieties have been carefully standardised so that they travel well, keep well in cold storage and have a good colour. I don't believe that most of them taste as good as the old ones, but they keep better, grow in a wider range of climates and look like what people now expect.

Up in our top orchard there is a massive, striped, yellow and green apple, which looks a bit as though it's suffering from elephantiasis, but it's the best cooking apple I've ever had. It melts to snow in the oven. It wouldn't sell because it doesn't look like an apple 'should'. In another orchard we have tiny freckled apricots which I have to persuade buyers to try; but once they have, they come back year after year. They have the most intense apricot flavour I have ever tasted.

Rogue trees are fun. Don't forget that the Granny Smith apple was a chance seedling.

Better stock

Grow lots of seedlings; select the ones that grow best, and you'll have varieties that grow well in your area. Most modern varieties are selected because they crop reasonably well over a range of areas. But they may not be the ones that do best where you are — so, experiment. Look for old trees in old gardens and take cuttings to keep regional varieties alive in your area.

Plant variety rights

Most seed sold today is hybrid, designed to fit the market. If you want plants to grow true-to-type, you have to continue buying from the seed companies as you can't save our own. Gradually, the old open-pollinated seed that you can save yourself is disappearing because of plant variety rights. By plant variety rights I mean that a variety bred by someone can be patented and royalties collected on the seeds. This is fair enough after the work put into breeding, but not if the only varieties sold are patented.

Sadly, this is becoming the case. Plant breeders are generally the companies that sell the seed, artificial fertilisers and pesticides. Many new varieties are bred to respond to large amounts of fertiliser and water, and also need pesticides and fungicides to keep them healthy.

This is not to say that all hybrid seed is bad. Much is excellent — some I grow every year. But the old open-pollinated plants are survivors. They are tough, and often more disease, drought, and pest resistant than hybrids are. They also produce over an extended season. Commercial hybrids are bred to bear all at once — excellent for the commercial grower who wants to harvest in a week, and free the land for another crop, but not for home growers who want to feed themselves for the entire year. Commercial varieties are bred for good appearance, and the ability to travel well and take cold storage — not primarily for taste. Many new varieties are actually more vulnerable to pests and weeds, and are lower in protein and vitamins than the varieties they replace. But they look better.

Gradually, old varieties are becoming lost or at least unavailable. This is our heritage — free seed, not seed that is chosen, packaged and sold to us. The only way that heritage will be preserved, for ourselves and our children, is if we learn to save those seeds and propagate such varieties ourselves.

Finding your plants

Gardens

Walk round the neighbourhood and look for plants that grow well in your area. Many gardeners carry a handbag or deep pockets in which to hide their cuttings, but it's best to knock and ask either for a cutting or some seeds. Few keen gardeners will turn away a fellow enthusiast. Offer to swap or to return some of the offspring, rather like the 'best of the litter' deals with animal breeders. Offer to prune old gardens and use the cuttings.

Parks

Collect seed, or even the odd inconspicuous cutting, from parks. Many Canberra rose gardens have been made by planting the old Parliament House rose garden prunings in winter. Seedlings in parks are usually rigorously pulled out or herbicided, so don't feel guilty snavelling a few.

Wander around your local parks when the gardeners are pruning the roses or other plants, and ask to take away some of the prunings. Rose prunings in particular are a great way to add to your collection.

If it tastes good, keep the seed!

Just about all fruit (with the exception of domestic bananas) and most veg grow well from seed. And yes, most will come fairly true-to-type too. (See chapters 3 and 4 on fruit and veg.)

Wild seeds

Collect seed in the wild. Do this only when there is no alternative — any seed you collect can't then germinate in the wild. Only take a VERY few seeds, and only then if there are many plants around. *Remember that it is illegal to take seeds or cuttings from a national park or reserve, so ask your local national parks office for permission first.*

Other sources

Many of our fruit trees came from the supermarket — we ate the fruit, then planted the seeds. This is a good, cheap way of getting fresh seed.

Seed doesn't have to be bought in neat packets. I've grown sunflowers from bird seed; millet from canary seed; soy beans from a packet bought in the supermarket (soak them first); buckwheat from the health food store; oats from horse fodder; wheat from uncooked whole wheat bought for topping bread; and maize from stud mix that passed through a horse into the mulch I put on the garden. I've grown peanuts from leftover, uncooked, unshelled peanuts I'd bought for chocolate chip biscuits.

Seed can be foraged. Look at supermarket shelves with a hunter's eye; look for fresh packets of whole seed. A lot of herbs grow from packets, as do most grains and many fruits.

Some propagation myths

You can't grow fruit trees from seed.

Nope. I've grown hundreds from seed. All have fruited — and most have fruited sooner than grafted, bought trees would have. All have come true-to-type too — pretty much like their parents.

It's faster to buy BIG plants from the garden centre.

Nope. (Unless it's a really massive plant costing hundreds or thousands of dollars.) Home-grown plants have less transplanting shock.

You need to spend lots of money on hormone rooting powders and stuff like that.

Nope. I don't bother. Neither do most home growers.

It's too hard!

Nope. I am possibly the least technically able person east of the black stump. If I can grow plants from seed or cuttings, anyone can.

Sources of non-hybrid seed

The following groups are helping to preserve our heritage — the species that are gradually disappearing from the world. Support them, and save your own seeds as well; even if you help save only one species from extinction, your efforts will be worth it.

AUSTRALIA

Seed Savers Network
PO Box 975, Byron Bay, NSW 2481
T/F 02 6685 6624 OR 02 6685 7565
E info@seedsavers.net
Website www.seedsavers.net

New South Wales

Henry Doubleday Research Association
C/- Lillian Osbourne
4 North Street, Mount Colah, NSW 2079

Extensive seed bank for members and others; quarterly magazine National Growing; exchange of information on saving seed and growing plants.

Daley's Fruit Tree Nursery
Daley's Nursery Lane, Geneva, via Kyogle
PO Box 154, Kyogle, NSW 2474
T 02-66321 441
Email donna@daleysfruit.com.au
Website www.daleysfruit.com.au

A superb range of really good-quality sub-tropical and tropical fruit, but I've grown a lot of their trees down here in the frosty chill. A great range of avocadoes, plus many unusual fruit, like chocolate sapote, tropical cherries, coffee bushes, and icecream bean tree. Ask for their free catalogue.

Honeysuckle Cottage
Lot 35, Bowen Mountain Road, Bowen Mountain, NSW 2753
T 02-45721345
Email kamcleod@zeta.org.au
Website www.honeysucklecottagenursery.com

Their catalogue has an enormous range of herbs, from tea bushes and anise sage to a vast collection of scented geraniums and violets. They also sell excellent bean seeds, and they have a superb rose catalogue.

The Gourdfather
PO Box 298, East Maitland, NSW 2323
T 02-4933 6624
Email gourdfather@kooee.com.au
Website www.thegourdfather.com

Fresh and dried gourds in a stunning collection of shapes, sizes and colours, books on growing gourds and what to do with them (A gourd banjo? Kids' toys? Grow your own storage containers?), and an extraordinary range of gourd seeds. Send them four 50-cent stamps for a catalogue.

Green Patch Non-Hybrid Organic Seeds
PO Box 1285, Taree, NSW 2430
T 02-6551 4240

Ring or write to find out when their next open day is or what their catalogue costs.

Queensland

Green Harvest
52 Crystal Waters, MS 16, via Maleny, Qld 4552
T 1800 681 041 free call, orders only
T 07-5494 4676 for general questions
Website www.greenharvest.com.au

The Australian Organic Gardening Resource Guide, their really superb, free catalogue, is the most comprehensive catalogue of its kind I know. I order from them regularly — everything from water chestnuts to nets for keeping out fruit fly, to really good-quality garden tools or a boracic acid puffer to get rid of silverfish.

Eden Seeds
MS 905, Lower Beechmont, Qld 4211
T 07-5533 1107
T 1800 188 199 free call, orders only
Website www.edenseeds.com.au

Great tropical and sub-tropical range, but I buy a lot of my cold-climate seeds from them too.

South Australia

Ross Roses
PO Box 23, Willunga, SA 5172
T 08-85562555
Email orders@rossroses.com.au
Website www.rossroses.com.au

Roses, roses, roses, including old toughies and the massive climbers I like to grow up fruit trees, plus all the superbly accurate information Ross Roses are renowned for.

Tasmania

Bob Magnus
C/- Post Office Woodbridge, Tas. 7162
T 03-62 674 430

A great source of rare and heritage apples, pears, plums and quinces, mostly grafted onto dwarf stock so you can fit more in a small garden. How about a fruit-tree hedge of a dozen different apples (Irish Peach, Macintosh, Sturmer Pippin, or giant Twenty Ounce cooking apples) along your front fence? Most of these are varieties you'll never see in a garden centre. Send them three 50-cent stamps for a catalogue.

Phoenix Seeds Association Ltd
PO Box 9, Stanley, Tas. 7331
M 004-58 1105

A not-for-profit organisation to counteract the disappearance of non-hybrid or specialty seeds. A wide range of unusual seeds. Write for their catalogue.

Victoria

Digger's Club
105 La Trobe Parade, Dromana, Vic. 3936
T 03-5987 1877

A wide range of hard to get and heritage seeds (like multi-coloured carrots, striped beetroot and black or yellow striped tomatoes) and ornamentals like tree dahlias. The first catalogue is free; after that you need to become a member, and once you pay your membership fees there are five catalogues a year. Non-members can buy plants at a higher price.

New Gippsland Seeds and Bulbs
PO Box 1, Silvan, Vic. 3795
T 03-9737 9560
Email newgipps@bigpond.com
Website www.possumpages.com.au/newgipps/index.htm

Free catalogue. Good-quality veg, herb and flower seeds and a great range of reliable and hard-to-get varieties.

Western Australia

Organic Growers Association of WA (OGAWA)
PO Box 7043, Cloisters Square, Perth, WA 6850
T 08 9498 1555
E enquiries@ogawa.org.au
Website www.ogawa.org.au
Permaculture Association of WA
Website www.permaculturewest.org

NEW ZEALAND

Seed Savers Aotearoa
Website www.seedsavers.org.nz

Koanga Gardens — Centre for Sustainable Living
Website www.koanga.co.nz

Tools to use

All you really need for propagating plants are your hands and a bit of soil, though there are some tools that make it easier.

Potting bench

This doesn't have to be a bench. I use a pile of old paving stones, the window-sill and a corner by the back door. But before you start potting up plants, work out where you are going to put them. Somewhere high is best — out of the reach of snails, dogs and cats, and away from feet that may trip over them. They should be warm but not in full sunlight; under a tree or awning is best. They also need to be near a hose or tap.

Pots

Anything that holds soil and allows drainage can be used. I use
- old cardboard (not foam) egg cartons (excellent for seedlings, just plant the whole container, well-wetted, or bung a hole in the bottoms);
- milk cartons (good for long-rooted tree seedlings);
- cracked teapots;
- an old milk churn;
- punnets that a friend brought us strawberries in; or
- tins with a few holes punched in the bottom.

Grafting tools

If you plan to do a lot of grafting, specialised tools are worth buying, though I've seen good grafters work with nothing more than an old, well-sharpened kitchen knife and some tape.

Any sharp knife can be used for grafting, but it must have a smooth, sharp edge — any small nicks or twists made in the plant can become infected. A straight knife is best. Polish the knife after every cut, if possible, on a clean cloth to stop it getting sticky and dirty.

A curved budding knife can be bought or can be made by grinding an ordinary table knife so that it is very sharp and curves slightly upwards.

Cutting tools

Cuttings can be taken with a knife or scissors, though many cuttings can just be snapped off with the fingers. Secateurs give a cleaner cut and don't tire the hands as much. The best secateurs have a curved blade closing on a straight blade.

Saws are good for large cuttings, like willows and poplars. Buy the best quality metal you can, as the saw will stay sharp longer and won't break.

Other tools

All gardeners acquire their favourite devices. I use an ordinary dessertspoon for planting out seedlings, or a hard, pointed stick. Most of my gardening 'tools' were never designed for garden use. I wrap my seeds in newspaper and store them in cardboard boxes from our local grocer. Even a spade isn't necessary if you have plenty of compost.

Useful bits and pieces are:
- a bucket for collecting compost materials;
- a wheelbarrow for collecting materials;
- old bits of sacking or material to shelter seedlings;
- old broom handles, straight sticks and other stakes for staking young plants;
- odd bits of string for tying plants;
- old stockings, cut into lengths, which make wonderful soft ties for plants;
- a good pair of scissors.

2 Basic Techniques

Once you're used to a few basic techniques you can grow anything. Though the techniques themselves are very simple, like anything else, the more expertise you gain, the more complicated the procedures you can tackle. However, just as not every musician gets to play with the Berlin Philharmonic, not every gardener will want to try very complex grafting techniques.

Don't forget that propagation techniques have been used for thousands of years by anyone who loved plants — well before the days of nurseries. It is only lately that these techniques have been handed over to experts, so don't be intimidated.

Cuttings

This is the easiest way of all to grow new plants. You just take a bit, put it in the ground, and wait for it to grow — in fact, many times it will be just that simple. Plants like geraniums (pelargoniums), wormwood, santolina and lavender rarely fail. Other times you will need to know what time of year to put the cutting in, or a few other details to help the cutting take.

There is another advantage to taking cuttings, apart from their simplicity. Seedlings vary; cuttings, grafted plants and divisions don't. Taking cuttings is the classic way to make a cottage garden. No need to time seed collection — just snip off a bit of any plant you fancy at the right time of year, bung it in the ground, and wait.

There is a lot of mystique about taking cuttings. Certainly, more complicated or sophisticated procedures give better results, but the cut-and-bung method will still fill your garden.

How to take a cutting

Take cuttings on a cool, wet or overcast day; this way they'll lose less moisture. Plant them as soon as you can. Any plant with a milky sap, though, like figs, frangipanis and cacti, should be left to dry for a couple of days to minimise the risk of rotting.

Use a sharp knife, if possible, or cut the end straight before planting. Loose bits can rot. If you're not going to plant straightaway, put the cuttings in a plastic bag and place it in the refrigerator; wrap the ends in damp newspaper; or put cuttings in a vase of water.

Where to plant cuttings

I plant my cuttings directly into the garden bed. This is fine as long as your soil stays moist (I put mine under the semi-shade of trees for added shelter), and is firm enough to hold the cutting up.

You do get better results, though, with sterile soil. Many cuttings will rot before they root, and sterile soil helps prevent this. You can use bought potting mix or make your own. Sterilisation is easy — just place the mix and a potato in a shallow tray in a conventional or microwave oven. When the potato is cooked your soil should be ready.

Classic potting mixes include:
• two parts soil, two parts sand and three parts peatmoss;
• half sand and half potting mix or soil;
• half sand and half peatmoss.
But any garden soil that holds moisture and doesn't cake will do, as long as it is sterile.

An easy way of planting cuttings is to press the cutting against the edge of a flower pot, then pour in sand. This way the cutting is held firmly, and the hard edge of the pot and the earth outside help to stimulate root development.

Planting out your cuttings

Remember that new roots are fragile; so treat them gently. Always wet them before moving, and choose a cool, dull day. They will probably need to be 'hardened off'. Don't plant out cuttings from indoors or shaded areas on a hot day, and don't plant cuttings grown in the warmth into cold soil. Choose a half-way place under the shade of a tree or on a verandah so that the plants gradually toughen up.

Never transplant too soon. Even though the growth on top of your cutting may be lavish, the roots may still be spindly — they may be able to take up nutrients without being strong enough to support the plant in the open. If the plant rocks at all when you press it, wait till it is firmer. Always stake plants from cuttings to cut down on 'wind rock'; as any movement will damage the young roots even more.

Sometimes a cutting shows very fast growth, with lots of leaves. Be wary. Pull it up and see if it has any roots; if it hasn't, throw it away. Cuttings that are slower, staying alive for some months without making new leaves, are probably establishing roots and will be hardier, more successful plants.

Softwood cuttings

Softwood cuttings are from young tender tips or new shoots, taken from either evergreen or deciduous plants, usually in spring. Take a few leaves as well as the shoots. Take them from the outer portion of the plant, which has more light, so growth is usually more vigorous. Cut a piece about 10 cm long as cleanly as you can from just below a node, with another couple above it. Leave a few leaves on the top of the cutting, stripping the rest away. This will help conserve moisture.

Keep softwood cuttings moist and humid with either a glass jar on top of the cutting or a plastic bag over the pot. They should strike within a week, or possibly two. Some cuttings need 'bottom heat' to strike. You can buy a special tray for this (though this is probably only worth it for the commercial grower), or you can make your own 'hay box' cutting table, as shown.

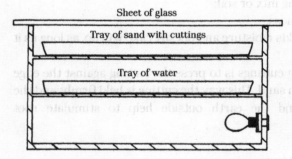

Sheet of glass

Tray of sand with cuttings

Tray of water

A home-made 'hay box' cutting table uses light bulbs to provide bottom heat for softwood cuttings. A more old-fashioned method is to fill the bottom cavity with decomposing hay, which gives off heat as it decomposes.

Semi-ripe cuttings

As shoots become firmer they are called semi-ripe — the wood changes colour from green to brown. These cuttings are taken later in summer, usually from evergreens. Treat them like softwood cuttings, though they should be a bit longer; say up to 15 cm. With cuttings from narrow-leafed plants like pines, take a heeled cutting; that is, a shoot that comes off a branch where you can take a small piece (a heel) of the branch as well. Don't remove the tip of softwood or semi-ripe cuttings as this contains hormones that help rooting. A semi-ripe cutting should strike in a month or two.

A heeled cutting also takes a small piece of the branch at the base of the cutting.

Hardwood cuttings

Hardwood cuttings are taken from wood that snaps, the previous year's growth that has hardened in autumn or more usually in winter when the plant is dormant or slower growing. They take longer than softwood cuttings to form new growth, as they aren't actively growing. On the other hand, they lose less moisture and don't rot as easily, so they usually root more successfully.

Make sure the cutting is straight to help stop rotting. If you want to take several cuttings from one stem, cut the tops at a slant. This way you know which end is up.

Hardwood cuttings vary from 60-centimetre branches (willows, poplars, olives) to small stems with three nodes. Hardwood cuttings may take several months to strike. One olive cutting I took remained dormant for 9 months; it was only left there because I didn't get around to moving it. Then, suddenly, it began to flourish.

Most hardwood cuttings take easily, just heeled into the garden and kept moist. You can improve their chances by putting a glass jar over them to increase heat and humidity, or a plastic bag if they are in a pot. Hormone dusts can be used, and will make the roots form sooner, but most cuttings take without them. I have never bothered with hormone dusts.

Most hardwood cuttings start to leaf in spring. Don't move them though, no matter how vigorous the growth. Give them time to form good roots.

To stop cuttings wilting before their new roots have formed, wrap the pot in a plastic bag, held up with two sticks.

Leaf cuttings

Leaf cuttings are just that — single leaves. Some plants such as cacti species and African violets naturally reproduce in this way, with the leaves rooting as they fall off each year. The leaf itself doesn't grow into a plant, but provides the food supply while roots form and a new plant grows beside it.

Leaf cuttings work best with fleshy-leaved plants like African violets, rex begonias and gloxinias. Place the leaves in damp sand, or sand and peatmoss. Otherwise, treat leaf cuttings like softwood cuttings, using hormone powder if you wish, and keeping them moist and humid. A fine cut through the veins in the back of the leaf will improve the chances of striking.

As most leaf cuttings are taken from indoor plants, they may be taken at any time. They should root in a few weeks.

Root cuttings

If you can get a piece of root without damaging the parent plant, place it lengthways in wet sand about 5 cm deep. Many plants grow from root cuttings, but this method is less popular than others because only a limited number of root cuttings can be taken without damaging the parent plant.

Layering

With layering the plant stays attached to its parent until new roots form. Sometimes this happens naturally (our kiwi fruit do it often, so does our Dorothy Perkins rose); you can also try azaleas, daphne, rhododendrons and sprawling roses.

A layered branch will develop roots where the stem touches the soil.

If you have good soil, just choose a pliable branch near the ground and cut off the leaves where it will touch the soil. Either bury the branch as it is, or make a cut on the bottom and press it into hormone rooting powder. Pin the branch firmly into the soil with a piece of bent wire or a stake. If your soil is tough and dry, cover the branch with potting mix instead. Keep moist and leave for anywhere from 6 months to a year, then sever the branch from its parent, and stake the new plant. Leave the plant alone to get used to its changed lifestyle, then move it wherever you want.

You can also layer plants into a pot. This is useful if you want to take them a fair distance to replant.

Air layering

This suits tropical and semi-tropical plants, and indoor tropicals like rubber plants. Air layering should be started in spring. Choose a stem from last season's growth. Cut away the leaves so you can make a cut in the bark about 20 cm from the tip and just below a node. The bark should be removed around the stem in a strip about 2 cm wide. Dust on hormone powder if desired, then wrap the area in damp (not wet) sphagnum moss, and tie it on with string. Now wrap up your parcel in plastic. You will be able to see the new roots form through the plastic, and the new plant can be severed in autumn.

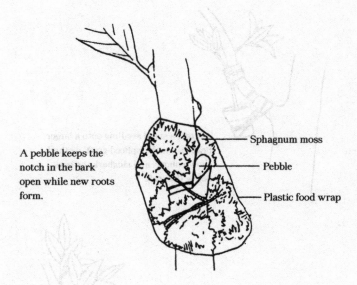

A pebble keeps the notch in the bark open while new roots form.

Sphagnum moss

Pebble

Plastic food wrap

Grafting

Grafting and budding are ways to join one plant to another. Grafting is a wonderful way to join a vigorous rootstock or disease-hardy rootstock onto the fruiting top you want, or to have two or more varieties grafted on one rootstock.

Grafting needs practice and dexterity. I am lousy at it. It is worth trying, however, even though budding is easier. If you're good at needlework, you'll probably be a good grafter. The techniques are simple — it's only the steady hand and good eye that are harder to come by.

17

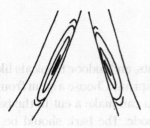

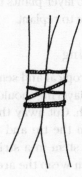

The 'spliced graft' method is the easiest graft of all – simply match the cuts and tie them together.

To graft a small seedling onto a larger branch, use the 'spliced graft' method shown above, and ringbark the bark below the graft

Sapling

Cutting

Keep the cutting moist in water while the cutting graft takes; then cut off the head of the sapling and the base of the cutting and seal with grafting wax.

Grafted plants must be compatible. Generally, this means the same sort of tree or plant, though a different variety. In practice the choice is wider. You can graft pear stock, for example, with hawthorn or medlar. Pears and apples can sometimes be grafted together, though different varieties are more successful than others. Plums can be joined with peaches, though their success and vigour again varies with each variety.

Even where the union appears to take, it can break some years later, as the two woods behave in different ways. Lilac can be grafted onto privet, though growth is usually short-lived but vigorous.

Even within the same group of trees there can be incompatibility. Persian walnut and black walnut, for example, may appear to take, then break down many years later.

The most important thing in grafting is for the two cambium layers to make contact so that the 'blood supply' of the top and bottom keeps on flowing. The second most important thing is to make sure the layers stay together by tying them properly.

Budding

There are several different ways of budding. The easiest is the T or shield bud. With deciduous plants, take a strong single stem in mid-winter and

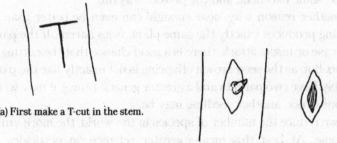

(a) First make a T-cut in the stem.

(b) Now cut a shield-shaped bud off a donor plant.

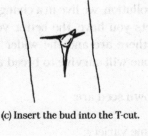

(c) Insert the bud into the T-cut.

(d) Bind the cut and bud with waterproof tape.

19

make a T-shaped cut between two buds. Now take a shield-shaped bud, loosen the bark on the cut with a sharp knife and insert the shield. Bandage the cut with waterproof tape (it is essential that no water or insects should be able to get in).

Keep the plant sheltered in the shade or under shadecloth for a couple of months till the bud takes. Once it starts to swell, remove the tape. As it starts to grow, take off any leaves or branches above or below the join.

Seed

There is one enormous advantage in using seeds; there are a lot of them. Even gardeners who aren't generous with their cuttings will usually give you some seeds.

Seed grows easily — after all, it evolved to reproduce plants without human intervention. But, unlike cuttings, seed-grown plants won't be exactly like their parents. This is not a major disadvantage for the home grower, as 'nearly' true-to-type should be good enough as long as seeds are chosen from the best plants, and you are careful not to plant seed from first generation hybrids. Even seed from a first generation hybrid can be fun. Once I planted seed from a hybrid broccoli; the offspring were nothing like the parent, but all were edible, some excellent, and the project was fun.

There is another reason why 'near enough' can even be better than 'the same'. A cutting produces exactly the same plant as its parent. If the parent dies from disease or insect attack, there is a good chance that the cutting offspring will too. But, as the seed-grown offspring is not exactly like the parent (it will probably have two parents and a greater genetic range), it may well be resistant. If one is not, another seedling may be.

The more we reduce the number of species in the world, the more vulnerable we become. At best this means greater reliance on pesticides and herbicides; at worst it can mean disaster from new conditions. Due to the greenhouse effect and other results of human pollution, we live in a changing world. It's a bit like a lottery — the more tickets you have, the better your chance of winning. So too, the more species there are and the wider the genetic variation, the more likely that at least one will survive to breed and spread again.

Some of the many reasons for raising your own seed are:
- to preserve old varieties;
- to ensure a wide genetic range within the same variety;
- to be able to grow different varieties not readily available in greengrocers, supermarkets and nurseries (not the same old silver beet, the same long

fat egg plant, the same flowers as everyone else because they were the varieties in punnets at the garden centre);

- because it's cheap;
- because its fun;
- because it links you with the unchanging pattern of growth from. the first life on earth;
- because home-grown seed is usually better than bought seed.

Most commercial seed is grown in only a few places – none of which will be like your garden. If you save seed from your own area you can save it from plants that do well there. After a few years you'll find your plants do better and better; you will have developed a strain exactly suited to your area and its requirements. Don't water much? Let the weeds grow up? Then the plants that do well for you will be ones that can cope with this, and their offspring should also be tough.

Packaged seed is readily available, though it may not be the sort of seed you want, or it may be too old. Some seed, like parsnip, usually fails to germinate after 12 months. While laws now ostensibly protect the consumer against non-germinating seed, in practice it is very hard to prove that your pumpkins didn't germinate because the seed had been badly stored or was too old. This year, for example, I grew about 120 different packets of seed, all from well-known seed companies. Three packets didn't germinate at all and seven had a very low rate of germination – apart from two cases where I bought the seed straight from the company, it may not have been the seed company's fault. Shops often store seed badly; it may have been subjected to too much heat or cold.

On the other hand, all of my own seed germinated. In fact, in 16 years I've never had home-grown seed not germinate, though I have had some odd results.

Choosing your seed plants

Choose the best plants for seed, not the ones that go to seed fastest as their offspring may go to seed quickly too. Place a stake near flowers you want, so that you know where they are. Stakes are also useful for keeping plants upright, as seed heads are often heavy; a fallen plant may cause the seed to germinate prematurely on the ground.

Always collect dry seed, fully ripe. If necessary, put a plastic bag over the seed heads in case it rains. Fertile seed is usually fatter than infertile seed. Keep your seed in a paper bag, in cardboard or in aluminium foil until it is to be used. Seed capsules or cones can be wrapped in newspaper, then put in a dry box. To obtain seed from pulpy fruit, soak the fruit in water then shake the jar till the seed floats to the top. Any seed that sinks probably isn't viable so you should throw it away.

Most seed can be sown at once. Some needs a dormant period, and some needs chilling before it germinates — such seed is usually from cold areas.

Don't collect seed from hybrid plants. To get the same plants again, you need to cross the same parents, and the parentage of most hybrid seed is hard to find out. Only plant seed from hybrids if you are prepared to accept considerable variation. Sometimes the second generation of hybrid seed is fairly true-to-type, but this won't happen in the first generation.

Collecting seed

Seed is produced at different times throughout the year. Most people know that fruit seed is ready when the fruit is ripe, but not so many people know when ornamental tree seed is ripe. Flower seed ripens after the flowers fall, anywhere from a few weeks to months later.

Seed can be taken from fruit, or shaken from old flowers; collected as it falls from a tree (either from the ground or from a tarpaulin under the tree); or caught in string bags placed around seed heads.

Storing seed

Seed should be stored in cool, dry conditions, such as in a paper bag or a sealed box. Don't store seed in glass jars — it may rot. Seed from fruit trees, or seed surrounded by pulp, should never be allowed to dry out; either store it in moist conditions or, better still, sow it at once. Apple seed, for example, germinates best as soon as it is taken from the fruit, as does orange, mango and avocado seed.

Large oily seed also doesn't store well, so sow it as soon as you can. Seed that is surrounded by oily pulp doesn't germinate till the pulp rots off or you scrape it off. Leave the seed in water to rot or, for faster results, feed it to animals and collect the droppings.

Use lavender flowers or lavender oil, dried garlic cloves or a bed of dried bay leaves to help keep weevils away from seed.

Stratification

Some seed must be kept moist between collection and planting, and some needs to be kept moist for chilling. Seed can be left in the refrigerator or outside in frosty weather. If outside, cover the pots with wood or a similar lid to keep mice and rats away.

If your plant originally grew in a cold area, like Northern Europe, the seed may need chilling to trick it into thinking that winter has gone and spring has come again before it will germinate.

Faster germination

If you want to speed up seed germination, soak the seed in water overnight. If seed has a waxy coating (like wattle seed), pour near-boiling water over it and soak overnight. Choose seed that sinks to the bottom. Seed with a tough shell can be placed in a jar containing a couple of centimetres of sand and shaken well, so that the shell is partially rubbed off to allow water to penetrate. Make sure the damage is not too deep as that might kill the seed. A large quantity of seed can be put in a cement mixer with sand and rubbed that way. Never let soaked seed dry out as germination will have begun. Plant the seed at once.

I germinate large seed by wrapping it in a damp towel and putting it in a plastic bag. I then put the plastic bag on the windowsill or by the stove (anywhere warm) and check it every few days. When the seed germinates, I plant it.

Towel

Seeds

Towel

Place seeds between two damp towels to speed up germination.

Seed-raising mixes

Bought mixes are free of weeds and disease, though ordinary garden soil can be used if it is sterilised. (Place the soil in the oven with a potato, and when the potato is cooked the soil will be ready.) A classic seed-raising mix is two parts good soil, one part peatmoss and one part sand. I have never bothered using peatmoss, though I do usually add some sand to my garden soil to lighten it.

Compost is excellent for seed raising, as long as you can be sure that it doesn't contain seed that will germinate (mine is often full of tomato seedlings and the odd pumpkin). If you have sand, add about one-third part sand to the compost to lighten it.

How to sow seed

Seed is, in a sense, hibernating like bears or lizards. Both the embryo plant and food reserves are stored in the seed: given warmth, moisture and oxygen it will start to grow. If any of these requirements are taken away — not enough oxygen (because of waterlogging), not enough moisture, or a cold snap — the plant will die.

Seed should be generally planted to a depth of about three times its size. Mix small seed with sand to spread it evenly.

Cover the pots with plastic bags or glass covers to maintain moisture, but remove the covers as soon as the leaves appear. Don't plant too much seed in a pot. Crowded seedlings don't do well. (I rarely take my own advice. Faced with too few pots and too much seed I always overcrowd, and always regret it.)

Containers

Seed can be sown straight into the garden. While this means it will be watered with the rest of the plants, and plants have room to stretch their roots, seedlings may also be vulnerable to weed competition, snails and other pests. Seed raised on a warm windowsill or patio will also grow faster than seed in a cold garden.

Seedlings can be grown in anything that gives enough root space and good drainage. Seedlings' roots should not be disturbed when planting out, and cramped punnets will mean spindly, weak plants. Old egg cartons, milk cartons and tin cans with holes punched in the bottom (or, better still, with the bottoms cut out and the tins stood on a wooden box so the plant and its bedding are easily removed) make excellent containers.

Fill each cup of the egg carton with soil and large seeds like zucchini, pumpkin, melon and cucumber. When they are ready to plant, soak the carton for 24 hours, separate the pieces and plant each section — soil, cardboard and all. Otherwise, tip the root-shaped soil sections out as gently as you can and plant them.

An egg carton is a cheap alternative to peat pots — just soak the carton, then plant the seedlings, container and all.

Cut the squares from the milk cartons and place them on a tray. Fill each square with potting mix and sow a maximum of four seeds — if the seeds are large, plant fewer.

Large, black plastic tree containers are perhaps the best — the black absorbs heat and snails don't like to crawl up them. A seed-raising bed made from an old tyre is also good — the black absorbs heat and the extra height means seedlings are slightly out of frost range. Drainage is excellent and as the beds are 'above ground', cutworms and other pests are less of a problem.

A friend raises his seedlings in old styrofoam boxes on a table. These have excellent drainage and the table helps keep them away from frost and snails. He labels each section of the box with a felt pen, and crosses out the old labels each time a new lot of seed is planted.

Peat pots are worth buying. The peat is broken down by the soil bacteria and you can plant pot and all without disturbing the seedlings — much the same as with segments of egg carton — just soak the pots overnight before planting.

Don't bother buying divided plastic pots with a segment for each seedling. The world doesn't need more plastic.

If you are reusing pots, wash them well and dry them in the sun to kill any disease. Try not to reuse terracotta pots as they can harbour bacteria. Heat terracotta pots in the oven if you want to use them. Never use broken bits of pot as drainage rubble in a new pot — you may be transferring disease.

Cliplock bags

I usually shy away from plastic. But these really do save time. Place a few handfuls of potting mix in the bag; moisten well; add seed or cuttings, then seal so the moisture doesn't evaporate, and store in a semi-shaded spot.
You will see when the cutting takes root or the seeds start to grow. Transplant them then, and reuse the bag. Saves a heck of a lot of watering and weeding!!!

Labelling

Always label your seedlings; I usually forget. This rarely concerns me now, but until you learn to tell cabbage from lettuce seedlings it may present problems. I use old iceblock sticks as labels, or arrange my pots in a line and list what is in each on a piece of paper to be kept indoors, for example: pot 1, spinach; pot 2, giant butter pumpkins. This is fine as long as my son doesn't pinch the paper to draw on.

Watering

Always make sure there are holes in the bottom of your pot for drainage. Wet instead of moist soil can mean your seedlings will rot as soon as they germinate.

If the seed is small, don't water it. Soak the pot in a bucket so the seed isn't disturbed, as it may splash out or clump together. Cover the pot with a plastic bag, but remove it as soon as the seedlings emerge so as to prevent fungus problems.

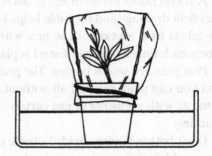

Watering pots can disturb seeds. Try soaking the bottom of the pot in a bucket or tray of water instead, so the water percolates gently upwards. Cover with a plastic bag to increase humidity, but take the bag off as soon as the seedlings appear.

Be careful when watering pots containing seedlings or you may wash the seed together or disturb young roots. Either place them in a larger pot of water so it is drawn up into the drier soil, or use a misting sprayer or very fine jet on the hose.

There's no such thing as overwatering until the seed germinates (though it may rot if drainage is bad and the water becomes stagnant in the pot). After germination, make sure the seedlings are kept just damp enough to keep them growing without surplus water remaining around them.

When to sow seed

Sow seed in spring and autumn if possible, rather than in the heat of summer. In very hot weather, try covering the seed with a layer of hessian or mulch until the shoots start to emerge, then remove the cover immediately. Seed doesn't need light, only heat, until it germinates.

Don't sow seed in saturated ground, as the soil is likely to form a crust over it. Seed will germinate faster in warm overcast conditions. Seed will also germinate quickly in rainy weather – even than if the pots had been kept just as wet. A wet January is a good time for sowing seed.

Seedling problems

Seedlings that wilt at soil level are plagued by damping off. If this is a problem, water once every 2 days with chamomile tea or garlic spray. An old-fashioned method was to soak two chopped garlic cloves per cup of water and water the seedling with the solution. Don't waterlog your seedlings; plants need oxygen. It is best to water in the mornings so that seedlings dry off before night, making them less prone to damping off.

Long, lanky seedlings don't have enough light, so move them. Pale green seedlings are starving, so add liquid manure. (This is made by covering manure or compost with water and draining off the coloured residue; weeds or refuse covered in water also make a good liquid manure.)

Wilting seedlings either need more water, softer light or less heat. Lettuce seedlings, for example, can cook and die in hot soil, even if it's wet.

If seedlings are cut at soil level, you have cutworms. Use a cutworm guard consisting of two toothpicks on either side, or cover the seedlings with an old tin can, open at top and bottom, or a section cut out of an old plastic soft-drink bottle. You can also wrap aluminium foil around the bottom of each seedling. Increase the humus level of your soil to inhibit cutworms.

Seedlings are very vulnerable to slugs, snails and cutworms. These can be deterred with collars from old tin cans (as described), pressed at least 5 cm into the soil. Tin cans also help shield the seedlings from heat, cold and wind. Remove the cans when the seedlings are growing strongly.

Keep snails away from your seedlings with a 'snail collar' made from an old tin can or soft-drink bottle.

Plastic bottles, with the bottoms cut out, can act as miniature greenhouses. Place one over each seedling. They also keep pests away.

Ant and mould repellent

Ants are often hungry for seeds in spring — and seeds sown into cold ground may rot. I roll my seeds in cooking oil, (fresh or used) then in a mix of one-half white or cayenne pepper or chilli powder, to keep the ants away, and one-half powdered milk, to inhibit moulds and rotting. Sow as usual.

Drought seeds

Seeds sown in a drought can be eaten by birds or ants, or they may germinate in the dampness from the dew then die from lack of soil moisture. Try planting them twice as deep as usual. Corn seed can be covered by up to 30 cm of sand — it'll take longer to germinate but the plants will be much more drought hardy.

No-dig pelletised seeds

If you want to 'broadcast' seeds — scatter them on bare or sparsely covered ground (i.e. tree seeds for re-treeing a bare paddock, or pasture seeds) mix 1

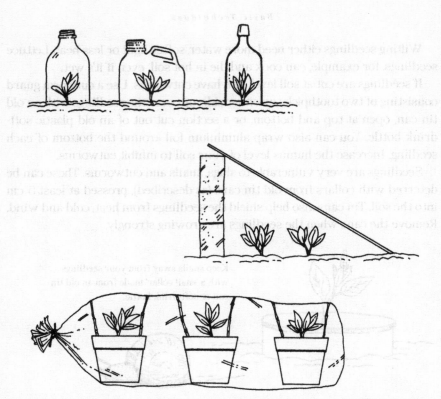

Home-made greenhouses can be old plastic soft-drink or cordial bottles, an old window, or a plastic bag held up with sticks.

cup of seeds with 3 cups of good loam (not sandy soil — it must have some clay in it and stay together when you clench a wet fistful) and half a cup of powdered milk. This can also be done by the spadefull in a cement mixer. (Clean it well first.)

The seeds will become 'pelletised' with a round covering of dirt. Spread them out, let them dry, then scatter them on top of the ground, preferably when rain is due — though that isn't essential, as they'll sit there for weeks or months until there's enough moisture to penetrate the covering of soil.

Reasons why seed may fail to germinate include:
- seed may have been old, infected with fungus or badly stored;
- seed may have been sown too thickly;
- seed may have been planted too deep; sow seed at a depth of roughly twice its size;
- seed may have been planted too shallow, causing the young shoot to burn off;
- birds or rats may have eaten the seed, or slugs or snails may have eaten the young shoot;

- seed may have germinated then died from heat or dryness;
- a hard soil crust may have prevented either shoots from breaking through or moisture from entering the root zone;
- soil may have been too loose and fluffy, so that the seed wasn't in contact with the soil moisture;
- watering may have been too heavy and washed the seeds to the surface.

Seed in the garden

Seed can be planted straight into the garden. Seed sown in the garden is less vulnerable to drying out than seed in smaller containers, and the seedlings' roots have more room to develop. However, seedlings are more vulnerable to pests and weed competition, and can easily be covered by larger plants, especially if you overplant. It is harder to dig seedlings out of a bed without disturbing the roots than it is to remove them from a small pot, where you can gently tip them (soil and all) into your hand.

Seedbeds should be in the best soil you have, well dug and weed-free, either with a sprinkling of dolomite and blood and bone or a good helping of compost. Rake the area before you plant it; seed will germinate more evenly and water won't run into rivulets and clump the seed together. Water with chamomile tea or garlic spray if you are worried about damping off. Never have undigested organic matter in the soil as the seed will rot. Mulch on the top is fine, but part it away from the seed until the seedlings are tough enough to snap, not bend.

Fine seed can be covered with hessian or newspaper for a week to stop it from drying out and from moving when watered. Sprinkle a little saw-dust, very well-rotted manure or old grass clippings as lightly as possible over the seed to stop the soil from forming a crust and to help keep moisture in.

I use sand to cover scattered seed. It's easy to sprinkle over, and much easier than pushing in each seed. You can also mix seed in a container of soil and sprinkle the lot over. Hand-driven seed planters are quite cheap and worth buying if you do a lot of planting.

Seedbeds are one area of the garden that shouldn't be mulched, at least not until the seedlings' stems are tough enough to snap; that is, they don't just bend when you pull them. Don't sow seed too thickly; even though seedlings have more room to spread, any tangled roots can still be damaged when they are dug up.

Birds like seed, so keep them away:
- Cover seedbeds with hen wire or shadecloth or, even better, with fine fruit fly netting. This should all be propped up at least a metre away from

the ground. (I use tomato stakes to keep it up.) Otherwise the seedlings may be bent or rot underneath where the cloth touches the ground.

- Pelletise seed (see above)
- Buy a motion-sensing scarecrow that shoots a jet of water at passing birds, possums or anything that moves. (Make sure the postman isn't in range.)
- Hawk kites, plastic snakes, recorded bird alarm calls, marbles rattling in old tin cans hung from trees, or the radio on a sport's channel will keep birds away for short periods of time. But birds are bright. They soon learn there's nothing to be afraid of. Of course by that time your seeds may have germinated. But if you need to deter birds for a long time, you need a permanent solution.

Hardening seedlings for transplanting

Give seedlings as much light and warmth as possible. If they need to be thinned, don't try to pull them out as you may disturb the roots of others. Snip them off with scissors. Try to leave at least 3 centimetres between each seedling; leave more if they will be advanced when you plant them out.

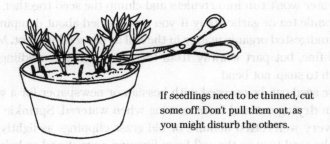

If seedlings need to be thinned, cut some off. Don't pull them out, as you might disturb the others.

Harden seedlings off gradually before they are planted so that you lessen setbacks. Place the plants in a sheltered spot in the garden for a couple of days. Bring them in if the nights are still cold; and make sure they are in broken light, such as under a tree, if the days are bright and hot.

Slice the seedlings as soon as they are a few centimetres tall, or have unfurled their first two leaves. Take a knife and slice vertically through the soil around each plant. Repeat when the seedlings are about 3 weeks old, and try to cut along the same line as before; it helps if seed is sown in a grid pattern, in rows.

Slicing cuts through any straggling roots and encourages the seedlings to make short bushy roots about the base, which are less likely to be disturbed when you transplant them.

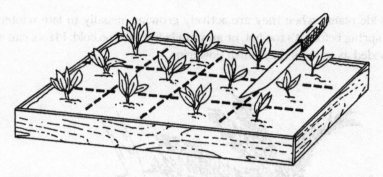

To encourage seedlings to make compact balls of roots that won't be disturbed when you transplant them, slice any straggling roots as soon as the seedlings unfurl their leaves.

Transplanting

Make sure the seedlings are moist before you transplant, and that the soil they are to be planted in is as moist and as loose as the soil the seedlings grew in.

Stake large plants as wind rock can kill them. Transplant on wet or cool days if you can, or shade them with newspaper or even an umbrella to minimise shock.

Watering is essential, not just to wet the soil but to fill up air pockets. Air round the roots means no moisture and no food, so poor plants.

Plant seedlings in the early evening, if possible, or sometime when it is cool, windless or (best of all) drizzling. Plants are rarely set back if planted when it is raining, even without any hardening off.

If you must transplant seedlings in hot, dry weather, try covering them for a short time with newspaper 'dunce caps', a clay flower pot (not a black plastic one as it will sweat) or even an umbrella.

If the roots have been damaged, pinch off enough of the top growth to compensate. Cut off about a third of lettuce and any other soft green foliage unless you are sure no root damage has occurred.

Division

This is one of the classic ways in which cottage gardens were propagated. Division means just that — dividing a clump which will then grow larger. Many ferns, including the common fish ferns and maiden hair, grow by dividing the clumps. You can also divide clumps of bulbs, which will then grow more vigorously with more room; or divide tubers or rhizomes, like potatoes or bits of ginger lily root, into small pieces, each with an eye that will shoot.

Divide plants when they are actively growing, usually in late winter or early spring before it's too hot, or autumn before it's too cold. Plants can also be divided as soon as they finish flowering.

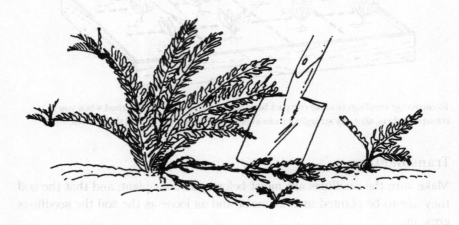

Divide ferns by cutting the rhizoids with a sharp spade.

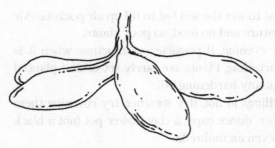

Dividing dahlia bulbs: select an old stalk, and separate each tuber to make a new plant.

Dividing a clump

The evening before you're going to divide, water the clump thoroughly. Choose a cool, dullish day if possible. Dig up the whole plant and separate it into as many sections as you want. These can be quite small, as long as each section has roots, stems and shoots. The plants furthest from the centre are usually the most vigorous.

Plants with rhizomes, like agapanthus, bearded iris and canna lillies, can have their rhizome chopped into small pieces, as long as each has a strong bud or tuft of leaves. Trim off any broken roots and leaves before replanting, as broken bits can rot and infect the rest of the plant.

Select a large clump

Dig out the whole clump
with as much soil and
roots as possible.

Pull it apart or, if necessary, cut
it into separate pieces with a
sharp spade. Plant the pieces in
new soil.

Runners

You'll know when you see a plant that propagates itself by runners — they
start spreading to look for new soil in which to root. Runners are usually
pulled up and planted in autumn, but can be transplanted at any time if they
have established their roots, and the ground isn't frozen or the day not too
hot. Strawberries are usually propagated by runners.

3 Vegetables

Most vegetables are easily grown from seed. Some also respond to cuttings, division or layering. Vegetable seed is easily collected, easily planted and easily stored, yet most vegetables grown in home gardens are still planted out from small plastic punnets of standard varieties sold at the garden centre.

Why grow from seed?

The seedlings you buy, prepacked and luxurious from greenhouses and the use of soluble fertiliser, are not necessarily the varieties you want to grow or eat, and may not have been grown in the way you'd prefer. The seedling industry makes its profit from 'reruns' — seedlings that die and are replaced. Punnet seedlings may look healthy, but very often they're not hardy. A day in the hot sun and they're dead, or they may be hunted out by snails tempted by their soft nitrogen-rich growth.

Commercial seedlings are rarely organic, they may introduce pests or diseases, they may be forced in glasshouses and not hardened off, or they may be too early or too late for your area. They are also expensive. While the cost may not be much per punnet, it can add up. Even a small vegetable garden needs at least twenty punnets per year; $50 buys only a few punnets, but a lot of seed.

The main reason I raise my own vegetable seedlings, though, and collect my own seed or use seed from seed banks or friends, is because there just aren't enough good commercial varieties to choose from.

Seed varieties are standardised, perhaps three varieties of tomatoes, one of silver beet, two of onions; and they may not be the ones that grow best in your area or that you prefer to eat. It reinforces the tendency in our supermarket-dominated society to accept an unvaryingly hard, pink tomato variety, for example, and shy away from diversity. I've seen children and adults wonder whether yellow zucchini, purple beans or white eggplant are edible, or what was wrong with silver beet with shorter, paler leaves than the commonly grown dark green and rather coarse Fordhook Giant.

I love round zucchini (wonderful dense, textured fruit that even kids adore, especially baked, or red freckled lettuce that survive our hot dry summers, or the yellow fleshed, red skinned carrots that take almost any amount of drought. And you just can't get those as punnets of seedlings.

Home gardeners are the major force in keeping some of the old-fashioned vegetable varieties alive — varieties that don't travel or keep well, or vary from the accepted vegetable norm.

Reasons for saving your own vegetable seed include:

- Saving money: one backyard can provide 95% of a family's food — for free, as long as you collect your own seeds.
- Increasing the availability of old-fashioned and non-commercial varieties.
- A sense of independence: I prefer the knowledge that my garden is independent of multinational packagers, seed patenters and chains of seed merchants.
- Personal satisfaction: when I look at the plants in my garden which I grew from seed, there is enormous satisfaction in knowing that they are mine — from seed to harvest.
- Better stock: when you keep your own seed and grow your own seedlings you can discard any weak seedlings, keeping only the strongest. In this way you can gradually build up a collection of plants which are suited to your area.

Collecting vegetable seed

Vegetable seed is free for the taking, but the taking is more difficult in some cases than others. If you want your veg to come true-to-type and not produce weird shaggy monsters instead of well-behaved cabbages, you need to know what you're doing. A bit, anyhow — and it isn't difficult. (Did anyone ever tell you about the birds and the bees as a kid? Well, this is the 'bees' bit ... how the bees, and a few other pollinators like wasps, beetles and some birds, help plants have sex.)

Plants have male and female bits. They are fertilised by the exchange of pollen from the stamen (male bit) to the stigma (female bit) of flowers. Some plants pollinate themselves. When this happens (and the plant is not a first-cross hybrid) the seed will probably produce a plant that is true-to-type.

When pollen is transferred between different plants, cross-pollination occurs. Offspring may be true-to-type if both parents were the same, but they won't be true-to-type if cross-pollination occurs between plants of the same species but different varieties. Some plants are both self- and cross-pollinated, either by wind or insects.

Most vegetable seed sold today is hybrid; it is produced by crossing different parents. Hybrid seed is more profitable to sell as it can be patented and many hybrids respond well to high levels of artificial fertiliser. By and large, the companies owning the seed rights also produce the fertiliser.

Some hybrids are excellent. Many aren't. They are sold because more money can be made from patented varieties, or because they have easily marketed characteristics — such as tomatoes that are round, firm and last forever, even if they have little flavour; or beans that crop in a couple of weeks and then are finished, which is excellent for the commercial grower who wants a large crop in a short time, but not for the home gardener who wants a long picking period. As a general rule, though, there are many exceptions. I find the old-pollinated varieties have a better flavour and texture than the hybrids and are more resistant to pests.

Most hybrid seeds are inbred to ensure the desired characteristics, and there is very little variation. Hybrid seeds are more vulnerable to new diseases or pests, simply because if one plant of one variety is susceptible, then all plants of that variety will probably be susceptible. I've noticed this with zucchini as well as a whole range of other vegetables. When one of my hybrid zucchinis gets powdery mildew they all get it, and die within a few days of each other. On the other hand, my open-pollinated plants are more variable. Some succumb early, some later, and some seem untouched. As a home gardener you should look for variations that show which plants suit your garden, and then keep seed from them.

Ensuring your plants are true-to-type

Self-pollinating plants should be grown at least 3 metres apart to ensure they grow true-to-type. Even then cross-pollination may occur, but it should be less than 1 per cent. Self-pollinators include lettuce, beans, peas and tomatoes.

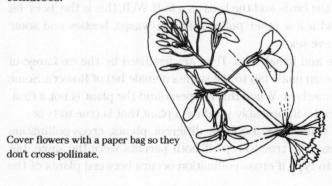

Cover flowers with a paper bag so they
don't cross-pollinate.

Cross-pollinating varieties need far greater isolation. It's hard to ensure true lines if plants of the same species are growing in the neighbourhood. You need about a kilometre between plants to be really sure, though as long as only one variety is flowering at any one time you are safe. As most gardeners don't let their vegetables flower (with the exception of plants like peas, beans and melons), you are usually fairly safe.

The alternative is to cover the flowers with paper bags during the pollination stage, and use a fine paint brush to brush the pollen over the stigma and stamens of each flower. Keep them covered till fruit begins to set. Sweet corn, beetroot, spinach and silver beet respond to this.

Actually, cross-pollination may not matter. In practice there may only be a few varieties of each vegetable in your district, so any cross-pollination may well produce an acceptable plant. With careful selection of only vigorous seedlings you may even come up with an improved variety.

Hybrids

Hybrids are the first offspring produced by repeated crossing of two or more parental lines. The next generation of seed is not true-to-type, and the variety may deteriorate rapidly — though you may not regard the change as deterioration. I find self-seeded, once-hybrid hollyhocks, for example, produce plants that I value more than the originals; they have small, single cups and clear, fine colours. However, as a general rule, it is a good idea not to save seeds from hybrid plants, as the results will almost certainly be unpredictable. Hybrids are usually marked as such on seed packets.

Selecting plants for seed

Choose only the best parents. Don't choose the first that go to seed, or you may find that their offspring also bolt early. With peas, beans and tomatoes, however, you may wish to encourage early seeders.

Processing and storing

Plants with fleshy fruit, like tomatoes, capsicums, melons, pumpkin and eggplant, are picked when ripe or over-ripe. The seed is scooped out, soaked till it is free, washed, cleaned and dried.

Dry seed, like beans, peas, corn, silver beet, spinach, carrots, lettuce and parsnip, should be allowed to dry on the plant. In wet weather, pull up the whole plant and hang it upside down under cover until the seed has dried out. Sun drying is best. Oven drying over 40°C tends to cook the seed.

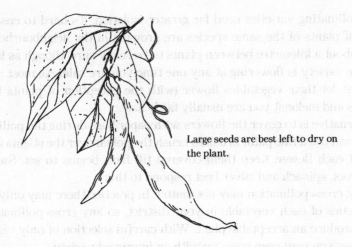

Large seeds are best left to dry on
the plant.

Dry the seed to as low a moisture content as you can, around 4 to 5 per
cent is best, with 15 per cent the maximum. Place it in a dry container and
store in a cool, dark place. Don't put seed in glass jars, as it will probably rot.
Wrap it in paper and aluminium foil, then store in envelopes or matchboxes.

Give the seed a viability test to check the level of germination. This can
also be done just after the seeds have been dried, so if most fail the test you
will have time to hunt out a new batch. To test viability, scatter a few seeds
on a damp towel. Cover with another damp towel and leave in a warm, dark
place for the correct germination time of the plant. (If you don't know the
germination time, hunt out a commercial packet of similar seeds and check
the time on the back.) Even if you get poor germination the seed may still be
useful. After all, it is free; just scatter it more thickly.

Rats and mice love to eat drying seed and can devour your entire supply
in a night.

Insect repellents to put with your stored seed include well-dried eucalyp-
tus leaves, dried cloves of garlic, bay leaves, dried cloves, lavender, pyrethrum
flowers, rosemary branches, tansy leaves and derris dust.

Commercial seed is usually treated with fungicides such as Captan. Fungicides shouldn't be needed if the seed is dry and well stored, but a little
powdered sulphur could be used as an alternative. A few grains of rice in
paper will absorb moisture.

Deliberate cross-pollination or hybridising

Seed can carry cells from two different plants – its parents. Each seed on a
plant isn't necessarily the same as any other seed from the same plant, even
though pollination may be by the same parent. However, the seeds should be

very similar. Seeds that are very similar to their parents are called true-to-type. The more the plants have been inbred to concentrate certain characteristics, the less variation there will be.

Some flowers have both stamens and pistils, and can pollinate themselves. When this happens, the seeds will be true-to-type, though in practice there is always a small amount of cross-pollination from wind or insects.

Other plants have both male and female flowers, and some, like asparagus, will have male and female flowers on different plants. Some plants, like avocados, have male and female flowers that open at different times, so that they must be cross-pollinated by a different variety. Cross-pollinated plants, of course, will vary more than plants that have been produced from one parent, but if both parents are alike the difference is small.

Remember that even true-to-type seedlings probably won't be exactly like their parents, though the difference may be so small that you won't notice it. The only way to get a plant exactly the same is to grow a bit of it, such as by cuttings, division or grafting.

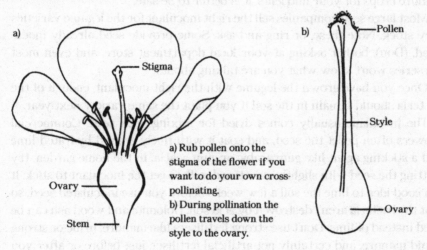

a) Rub pollen onto the stigma of the flower if you want to do your own cross-pollinating.
b) During pollination the pollen travels down the style to the ovary.

In general, seed from one parent will be almost identical to that parent; seed from two similar parents will be very similar; and the more inbred the plants, the more similar the offspring will be — and most modern varieties are severely inbred to get the desired characteristics. Plants closely related to each other, but not of the same species, may also be mutually fertile. In this case, some of the offspring will resemble one parent or the other, and some will not look much like either.

If you want to cross-pollinate, you will need to transfer the ripe pollen of the male to the female. Look for pollen-bearing stamens. Pick them out with a pair of tweezers and transfer the pollen to the stigma below. This should be done when the stigma are tacky to touch, so the pollen will stick. If it doesn't stick, try again in a day or two. When the ovary (the seed pod) is ripe, the seeds inside will contain the characteristics of both parents. But you won't know which characteristics until the plant grows. Remember that the more similar the parents, the less change there'll be in the offspring.

Inoculating legume seed

The ability of a legume to supply nitrogen to the soil depends on its association with certain bacteria called rhizobium. These stimulate the roots to form nodules in which the bacteria multiply. Neither the plant nor the bacteria can fix nitrogen by itself.

No grower should take it for granted that the right bacteria will be in the soil at the right time and in the right place. If you want the best results from your legume crops or are relying on nitrogen-fixing bacteria and green manure crops for your nutrients, it is better to be safe.

Most large seed companies sell the right inoculant for the legume varieties they stock. Note these, or ring and ask. Some provide seed already inoculated. (Don't bother asking at your local department store, and even most nurseries won't know what you are talking about.)

Once you have grown the legume with the right inoculant, enough of the bacteria should remain in the soil if you plant the same variety next year.

The inoculant usually comes dried for mixing with seed. Commercial growers often pellet the seed, and coat it with finely-ground hydrated lime and a sticking agent like gum arabic or gum acacia. In the home garden, try wetting the seed with slightly sweetened milk to get the inoculant to stick. It is a good idea to lime the soil a few weeks before you use inoculated seed, so that the bacteria aren't destroyed by acid soil. Dolomite and wood ash can be used instead of lime. Don't use strong fertilisers like manure, urine or strong liquid manure, and certainly not artificial fertiliser, just before or after you use inoculated seed. Leave a few weeks' breathing space.

Don't expose inoculated seed to sunlight more than is necessary, as sunlight will kill the bacteria.

The following crops benefit from inoculation: peas, beans, broad beans, soybeans, lucerne, clover, vetch, lupins, mung beans, peanuts and tree lucerne.

An easy seed regime

It's easy to collect most of your seed; it's only when you try to collect every bit that it becomes exhausting. I limit myself to collecting seed that is simple to save; that is expensive to buy; that needs to be fresh; or that I particularly value and can't get any other way.

The most expensive seeds are peas, beans and broad beans, because of their weight and bulk. Luckily, these are perhaps the easiest for the home gardener to collect and store. Pumpkins, melons and zucchini are probably the next most expensive but are also easy to collect. Corn is more of a problem, as it is difficult to get a non-hybrid variety and it cross-pollinates easily. But unless you are in a country district where someone is growing maize, cross-pollination shouldn't be a problem for home consumption.

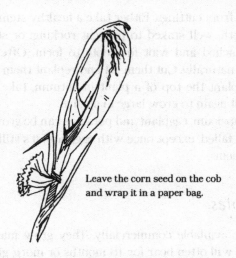

Leave the corn seed on the cob
and wrap it in a paper bag.

Some seed I always let self-sow, with patches of plants springing up, virtual perennials, that I need do no more to than pick and thin out. Radishes, parsnips and foliage turnips need a lot of thinning out. For slow germinators like tomatoes and carrots, you need to mark a place to leave vacant or they may get crowded out by spring growth.

The following plants can all be left to go to seed, with the seed falling and germinating naturally so you can pick the result: carrot, silver beet, radish, beetroot, parsnip, celery, daikon or long white radish, spring onions, foliage turnip, parsley, leek, Chinese cabbage (not true-to-type), Italian parsley, red and green mignonettes, cos lettuce, turnip-rooted parsley, hollyhocks, cornflowers and calendulas.

In practice, these get shifted round the garden as seed blows or as I transplant the surplus elsewhere. These self-seeding patches are my most productive part of the garden. The plants are hardy and self-selected to be best suited to this area. They grow and propagate with minimal attention — just a few loads of mulch to keep down the weeds and keep up a good supply of slow-release nutrient.

While tomatoes self-sow without encouragement, they should be transplanted because of the risk of disease. A strong garlic spray on the stem and soil when the tomatoes are young may prevent disease. One neighbour kept her tomatoes in the same place for over 12 years. She had a hen run just above, so seed and manure washed down into the garden; it was the most luxurious garden I've ever seen.

Vegetables from cuttings

Tomatoes grow easily from cuttings. Either take a healthy stem and plant it to about a hand's depth, well staked to prevent rocking; or stake down a branch while still attached and wait for roots to form. Often, sprawling tomato branches root naturally. Cut them off and replant them for a succession of tomatoes, or plant the top of a plant in autumn, take it inside for winter, and plant it out again to grow large in spring.

I have heard that capsicum, eggplant and potatoes can be grown from cuttings. I have tried and failed, except once with eggplant. It's still worthwhile experimenting with them.

Grafted vegetables

Grafted tomatoes are available commercially. They grow massive, and if planted in a mild spot will often bear for 18 months or more, giving a much earlier crop in the second year. Beware, though — a lot seem to be badly grafted and the graft may break down. The rootstock also seems to be simply too vigorous, and many — if not most — growers find that they get large crops of hard, barely edible small fruit, while the grafted bit vanishes.

It is very easy to graft your own tomatoes. Choose a vigorous rootstock, like tiny Tim or cherry tomatoes that are cold-tolerant, or a climbing tomato, and graft on your favourite variety. I have heard of tomatoes being grown on native solanums like wombat berry, which is frost-tolerant, and they produced for about 3 years. Tomatoes can also be grafted on to potatoes for a double crop, though the only time I tried it I got fewer tomatoes and fewer potatoes than from other plants nearby. However, I am a clumsy grafter and perhaps my plants were set back. Someone with a more delicate touch may have better luck.

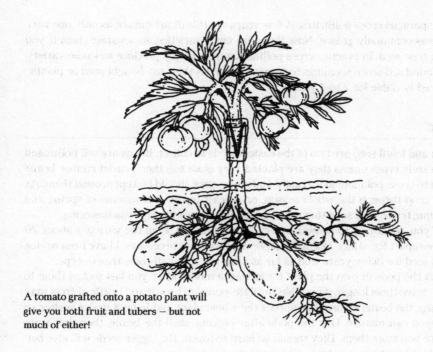

A tomato grafted onto a potato plant will
give you both fruit and tubers — but not
much of either!

Vegetables for seed collection

Artichoke

Artichoke seed is easy to keep. Let the artichoke grow until the thistle-like seed turn
fluffy and can be easily pulled out, or keep the whole dry head in a paper bag. Sow
in spring.

Artichokes are usually self-pollinating, and I have found they come true-to-type,
though others have found a lot of variation in seedlings (possibly they are becoming
more uniform with inbreeding). Artichokes grow very quickly from seed and will
often fruit in the first year. They germinate easily, so just pull out any that don't
thrive or produce good fruit.

Seed is viable for at least 2 years, probably more.

Asparagus

Asparagus plants produce seed from 2 years old — a lovely dance of bright red berries among the fern. Pick the berries when soft and red, mash them, wash the seed
away from the pulp, dry in the sun for a day, then move the seed to a dry spot
indoors for a couple of weeks. Alternatively, soak the red berries for 3 days then
plant straight away. The berries are borne on the female plants; the male plants produce thinner stalks.

Asparagus cross-pollinates. A few years ago this didn't matter, as only one variety was commonly grown. Now there are more varieties, so separate them if you want true seed. In practice cross-pollination may simply produce welcome variety. I've found self-sown seedlings to be more vigorous than any bought seed or plants.

Seed is viable for 2 to 3 years.

Bean

Bean and lentil seed are two of the easiest seeds to collect. Beans are self-pollinated and rarely cross unless they are planted very close together. Scarlet runner beans seem to cross-pollinate more easily, and more space should be kept around them. As they crop through the whole season, or at least in the cool months of spring and autumn, try to save seed that set when no other bean variety was flowering.

If you are trying to protect a very rare bean seed, keep the varieties about 20 metres apart for safety. Normally, however, this is not necessary. I have been saving bean seed for many years; and as far as I can tell, it has all come true-to-type.

Let the pods dry on the plant for at least a month after you last picked them to eat — leave them longer, if possible, until the pods are brown and brittle. If frost may damage the beans before this, uproot the whole plant and hang it under shelter so the seed can mature. Dry the pods after picking, shell the beans, then dry again before you store them. They should be hard to touch. The bigger seeds will give better plants next year as they will have larger food reserves.

Store bean seed in paper or cloth bags or old matchboxes; not in airtight jars as it may rot. Bay leaves, lavender or garlic cloves will help keep away weevils. Large amounts of seed can be stored in dry wood ash to keep away rodents.

Seed is viable for 2 years, though I have kept germinated seed in a matchbox in the cupboard for 6 years.

Beetroot

Beetroot is wind-, and sometimes insect-pollinated. It needs up to one kilometre separation between varieties. Never collect seed from plants that bolt up in the first year — wait till spring.

Beetroot cross with silver beet, so don't let them go to seed at the same time. Cut off the silver beet flower heads until the beetroot is finished.

Seed is viable for 3 years.

Brussels sprouts

See Cabbage

Cabbage (Red cabbage, savoy cabbage, brussels sprouts, broccoli, cauliflower, Chinese cabbage)

Most of these readily cross with each other. They are pollinated by insects and need a good kilometre between varieties to ensure they grow true-to-type. Otherwise, you may find you have peculiar cabbage-brussels sprout or broccoli-cauliflower off-spring. I have collected cross-pollinated seed several times. All the results were strange — including a brussels sprout plant with a cabbage top as tall as my waist, and soft, loose cabbages that went to seed without heading. In spite of their appearance, all were edible, though not good enough to warrant keeping the strain.

If you want to keep seed in the home garden, the best way is to only grow one variety for seed a year. You can also make sure they don't flower at the same time by cutting the flower heads off. Otherwise, try pollinating them by hand. Cover the flower head with a paper or calico bag stretched over wire; staple it onto the plant. When the flowers are open, take off the bag, brush the flowers with at least three other flower heads, then replace the bag.

Seeds are viable for 3 to 5 years.

To prevent seed-borne cabbage disease, immerse the seed in hot water at 50°C for 15 minutes before you dry it for storage

Capsicum

See Peppers

Carrot

Carrots are insect-pollinated and need about a 100 metres between varieties. Let seed ripen on the stalks and store without threshing in paper bags. I have let my carrots cross-pollinate haphazardly for about 10 years; the resulting carrots are hardy, long, pale orange and sweet. (I also grow several heritage varieties, like white and yellow carrots, and a very hardy yellow carrot with a red skin. All these are much more drought hardy than commercial carrots). Carrot seed usually matures in late summer, which is too late for self-sown carrots unless you choose an all year round variety.

Seed is viable for 1 to 3 years, depending on the variety.

Cauliflower

See Cabbage

Celery

The only way I can grow my own celery is to let it self-seed; seed sown in our cool springs takes too long to germinate. Celery is insect-pollinated so different varieties will cross. In the home garden this probably doesn't matter, as varieties are not likely to be flowering at the same time, and any cross will probably be good anyway. However, celery can cross with celeriac, so don't let them flower at the same time. Just cut back the celery flowers until the celeriac is finished; more celery flowers will keep coming.

Don't collect seed from plants that go to seed in the first year, but rather choose the latest plant to seed in spring.

Be careful harvesting celery seed. Once it is ripe, it falls quickly. Use a newspaper spread over the ground to catch it.

The seed is viable for 3 to 5 years.

Seed-borne celery disease can be prevented by immersing the seed in hot water at 48°C for 15 minutes before you dry it for storage.

Chicory Chives

See Onion

Choko

These are usually self-pollinating plants, though, to be sure, keep different varieties slightly apart. Treat them like lettuce seed.

The choko seed is in the choko. Chokos need to be fully ripe before you pick them for sprouting. Leave them in a dry dark place until the new shoot starts to poke out of the centre of the top of the fruit, then plant the whole fruit in a frost-free spot.

Choko seed only keeps till the next spring; and often not that long. If chokos start to sprout early, slow them down in the refrigerator, or plant them in a big pot on the windowsill or patio until the frosts are over.

Corn (Sweet corn, maize, ornamental corn)

Corn is wind-pollinated, and requires at least 70 metres between varieties, though if you grow your corn in a tight bunch with a trellis of beans between it and the next lot, the seed from the innermost plants may be good. I often grow sweet corn as well as maize (which sprouts from the mulch) and ornamental corn. Even with a lot of care I often get cross-pollination, though some years, with no care at all, seed I've kept for the chooks has accidentally sprouted and turned out true-to-type.

You can also separate corn varieties by weeks, instead of space, by planting early, mid- and late-season varieties. However, unless you are isolated, the corn may still cross with your neighbours.

Corn can be easily hand-pollinated. As soon as you can see green tassels through the papery leaf coating, put paper bags over the cobs (not stockings as the pollen can blow through them). As the tassels develop in the bag, they will shed pollen that can be collected each evening or during the day. Sprinkle this pollen on the other tassels. Make sure you put the paper bags back so that no outside pollen gets caught on the tassels. This means that your patch of corn only breeds with itself – not with pollen blown in from elsewhere.

Let the cobs ripen fully before you pick them. Corn is ready for seed about 3 to 5 weeks after it is ready for eating – the kernels will look slightly shrivelled.

Maize and ornamental corn are much harder and flourier than sweet corn, though both can be eaten when young and tender. Even if you do end up with a sweet corn-maize cross, you can still eat the result – but it will be very tough and dryish unless you pick the cobs when they are quite immature. I once had a cross that tasted like sweet corn with the colour of ornamental corn; it was good to eat, but few guests were game to try blue, red and orange corn.

Let the ears dry on the stalk. I'm lazy and store the whole ears dry in paper bags, scraping the seed off only when I want it. Seed can be easily removed from the cob.

Most commercially available corn varieties are hybrids. Beware: it's not worth-while saving seed from them unless you are prepared for the offspring to be radically different from the parents.

Seed-borne corn disease can be prevented by soaking the seed before sowing in a solution of 25 g copper sulphate to 1 litre of water.

Cress

Cress plants will cross, but there is unlikely to be more than one variety nearby. Seed can mature at any time in warm weather, so you may get a few harvests a year.

Cucumber

Cucumber should be slightly yellow, almost rotting before the seed is ripe. Don't worry if the frost gets them, they'll just rot quicker and the seed will be easier to wash out. Don't let the cucumber go brown though; it should still be whole and yellow.

Scrape the seed out into a jar and ferment it for at least a week, stirring every day until it sinks to the bottom. Wash the seed and dry it in the sun.

Cucumbers are insect-pollinated and cross easily. You probably need about 100 metres between varieties, or you may end up with interesting crosses between long green and apple cucumbers, and others. Again, make sure you don't save seed from hybrids; I have tried, but always with bad results.

If you want to grow several sorts of cucumber, cover the flowers with a paper bag and fertilise them yourself with a thin paint brush, or by rubbing one or two male flowers over the female flowers.

Seed is viable for 5 to 10 years.

Dandelion

These are usually self-pollinating, though to be sure, keep different varieties slightly apart. To be safe, mow wild dandelions in the lawn while yours are flowering so that they don't cross-pollinate. My dandelions have improved with selection, as I have rooted out all but the best over the past few years.

Seed is best used within 2 years.

Eggplant

Eggplant is self-pollinated and insect-pollinated, so crosses with other varieties are possible. Keep at least 20 metres between varieties to be sure, though for home use any crosses will probably be good.

Eggplant needs to be over-ripe for seed collection, starting to turn almost pale again after being almost blackly purple. The seed inside will be hard and black. Scoop out the seed, wash several times to free it from the flesh or ferment the flesh for a couple of days until the seed comes free, then dry as quickly as possible in the sun to prevent germination.

Eggplant that has been picked and allowed to shrivel in the cupboard will often have produced ripe seed in the meantime.

Seed is viable for about 3 years.

Endive

Endives are self-pollinating. Harvest the seed heads when the hulls are dry and crisp.
Endive seed is viable for 5 to 6 years.

Garlic

Garlic rarely sets seeds. When it does you can plant it, but you will get much smaller bulbs than if you planted a clove. Cloves are best planted in autumn for larger bulbs, but can really by planted any time when the ground is warm.

Kohlrabi

Most of these readily cross, and a good kilometre is needed between varieties to ensure they grow true-to-type. On the other hand, only one variety is likely to be flowering at any time.
Seed is viable for 4 to 5 years.

Leek

See also Onion. I always leave a few leeks in the garden to go to seed, and let the seed fall naturally to grow into large clumps of slender, tender leeks around the old plant. I save other seed to plant in spring to get the really fat leeks.
Leek seed is viable for 3 years.

Lentils

See Bean

Lettuce

These are usually self-pollinating, though to be sure, keep different varieties slightly apart. Again, with lettuce, don't select seed from early bolters. The stalks of seeding lettuce may need staking to stop the plant from falling over. Lettuces are prolific seeders; one plant can produce 30 000 seeds. Save seed from a few lettuces and mix it to increase your gene pool. I generally have lettuce varieties that will grow all year round, like red and green mignonette. One or more varieties are usually going to seed, with the seed falling naturally; this way there is always a succession of lettuces.

Let lettuce seed dry on the plant till the hulls are crisp. Cut off the dry stalks and keep them in a paper bag, or crush the pods and keep the seed inside.

Lettuce seed is viable for about 3 years.

Maize

See Corn

Melon (Rockmelon, watermelon, mini melon, honey dew melon)

Watermelons won't cross with rockmelons, but other varieties cross easily. Melons are insect-pollinated. To be sure, you need about 100 metres between varieties, though in practice any reasonably separate melons will be safe. Always collect melon seed from non-hybrid varieties, and make sure you don't have two varieties intertwining.

My melon crosses have always been bad. Once I had a wonderful crop that was completely bitter, and another lot was tasteless. Melon seed will germinate as soon as the melon is sweet — plants don't have to go soggy-ripe like cucumbers and zucchini. You can either spit out the seeds as you eat the melon, or scrape them from the centre. Dry them and plant in spring. However, you will get better germination and keeping if you put the seed with a little pulp in water for a week until it ferments. Rinse the seed well, dry it and store in a sealed container.

Melons can be hand-pollinated if you want to grow several varieties. Try to pollinate the first female flowers — they will be the ones that look bulbous round the base, as though they have small fruit there. Rub them with a few male flowers, then cover with an old stocking round a wire coat hanger until the fruit has set. Take the stocking off before the fruit gets too large. Not all flowers set on melons anyway, so be prepared for at least a half to two thirds to fall off.

Mustard

Mustards cross-pollinate, so you will need a good kilometre between varieties to ensure they grow true-to-type. Both black and white mustard seeds are sold. However, mustard is a rare crop in suburbia, and you may be lucky enough not to have anyone near you who's letting mustard flower.

Okra

This is mostly self-pollinated, but if you want to be really sure of a pure strain, cover the plant with a paper bag or nylon stocking so that it is pollinated with its own pollen. Collect seed from the pods. Cut away the flesh and dry the seed in the sun.

Onion (onions, chives and shallots)

Onions are insect-pollinated, and need at least a half a kilometre between varieties to be sure they don't cross (though in the home garden you could take a punt that no one else in half a kilometre will have onion flower heads at the same time). I have found that separating different onion varieties using trellises with climbing peas and beans is enough to ensure reasonable true strains for home use.

Onions are biennial. Leave the bulbs in the ground or plant them again in winter to re-sprout. They may need to be staked once the seed head forms so that they don't fall over. You can also plant bought onions and let them seed. Onion tops will sprout and may form a seed head, but probably won't be sturdy enough to carry a seed head without falling over. However, you can try.

Pick onion seed as soon as it turns black and starts to fall out of the seed head. Do this at once, as onion seed falls quickly when it's ripe and you may lose it.

Seeds are viable for 2 years.

Leeks may cross with onions. If you have both flowering at the same time, use paper bags and a paint brush as before, though, in the home garden, an onion-leek cross may be interesting and even worth trying to achieve.

Separate onion varieties so that they don't cross-pollinate. Place a trellis of climbing beans or peas between them.

Parsnip

Parsnips need isolation from other varieties, but no one else is likely to be growing any and there is little range on the market. Even when you do get a cross you may not notice. I always let my parsnips self-seed — a seed head in autumn, well staked, will still be dropping seed in spring. Parsnip seed is only viable for one year, which is why many people have trouble with germination. The trouble isn't in your gardening methods, so forget about putting hessian, etc. over parsnip beds to help the seeds along — you just have dud seeds. Fresh parsnip seeds grow like a weed, and can become one.

Pea

Though sometimes insect-pollinated, peas are self-pollinating and the seed is easy to collect. Leave a few metres between varieties in case of insect pollination, though by and large seed seems to be true-to-type. Let pods dry on the plant. Pick the pods, dry in the sun for a few days (don't leave them in the dew or rain), pod the seed, then dry again.

Seed is viable for 2 to 3 years.

Pepper

Peppers usually self-pollinate, but sometimes insects pollinate them as well and crosses are possible, though not likely. Chilli peppers cross-pollinate more easily than sweet ones, so keep them about 20 metres away from other varieties.

Make sure capsicum and peppers are as ripe as possible, almost rotting, before you use them for seed. They need to be washed and dried quickly to prevent germination; sometimes you will find a capsicum seed that has germinated in the capsicum. Use the same separation technique as for tomatoes to prevent disease, though seeds just scraped out and dried and stored in an envelope are fine for home use.

Seed is viable for 3 to 5 years.

Potato

Potato seed, the berries on top of the plant, aren't seed potatoes. Seed potatoes are disease-free potatoes planted to grow more potatoes.

There are conflicting reports about potato seed: some people say it isn't fertile, while other gardeners claim to have grown it. (I have done so once.) I suspect that fertility varies. Seed does definitely grow, as new varieties of potatoes are grown from cross-pollinated potato seed.

Planting potato seed is much slower and more inconvenient than planting tubers, but if you have been growing two varieties next to each other, or pollinate the flowers yourself, you may get a new variety. Try and see. (Remember: the berries are very poisonous — don't leave them where children may eat them thinking they are fruit.) Plant seed in spring. The potatoes produced from potato seed plants are very small, but can be planted the next year to get bushes with good-sized potatoes.

Radish

Most radishes cross readily, and you need a good kilometre between varieties to ensure they grow true-to-type. In practice, this may not matter to the home gardener. My radishes have been self-sown for 16 years, and have grown hardier and lustier. Even though there are at least three sorts growing at any one time, none appears to have cross-pollinated.

Radish seed forms prolifically in capsules. Pick these capsules when they are pale yellow and dryish; keep them in paper bags till spring or shake out the seed and store that.

Seed is viable for 5 years.

Rhubarb

Rhubarb seed is easy to collect, but plant division is an easier way to get plants true-to-type, especially if you don't know if your rhubarb plant is a hybrid (even many nurseries don't know what variety of rhubarb they are selling). Still, seedlings are a fast way to get a lot of rhubarb plants, and you can always pull out those that don't do so well. Never collect rhubarb seed from a plant that goes to seed early or often, or your new plants may do the same.

Seed is viable for 5 to 6 years.

Salsify

Salsify self-pollinates. Pick the seed as it ripens over summer; don't wait till it all ripens or it may shatter and you'll lose some. Dry the seed for 2 weeks before storing.

Salsify seed is viable for only 1 year; if you want good germination you need to save your own seed and use it fresh.

Shallots

See Onion

Silver beet

Silver beet is wind-pollinated, and needs up to a kilometre between varieties. Never collect seed from plants that bolt in the first year — wait till spring. The seed is easily collected in spring, or you can dig up the plants as they go to seed and hang them upside down, with a paper bag over the top, and collect the seed in that way.

Silver beet cross-pollinates with other silver beet varieties, but only three varieties are easily available and only one is common. Any crossing will probably give you good silver beet. Silver beet can also cross with beetroot, but this is fairly rare.

Seed is viable for 3 years.

Sorrel

Fresh sorrel reseeds itself naturally all over the garden. It will cross-pollinate with other varieties, so theoretically a cross with wild sorrel may be possible, though I haven't seen it happen.

Seeds are viable for about 3 years.

Spinach

Spinach is wind-pollinated, but it is unlikely that more than one variety will be grown near you. Pick the seeds as they ripen and turn black. Pull out any plants that go to seed early so that they don't pollinate any of the later ones, producing off-spring that bolt early the following year.

Squash

See Zucchini

Sunflower

Sunflowers are usually-self-pollinating, but can also be insect-pollinated. To be sure, keep different varieties apart. Sunflowers may cross with other varieties nearby, but usually don't. I have found mine true-to-type, even though I grow two varieties close together.

Seed is viable for at least 3 years.

Tomato

Tomatoes are self-pollinating, unless you have two varieties growing right next to each other (even then seeds will probably be true-to-type). If you want to make sure that rare varieties don't cross, have about 50 metres between them.

Let tomatoes get squashy ripe, scoop out the seed into a glass jar and ferment it for about 5 days. The fermentation isn't necessary for the seed to germinate, but will help keep it free of bacterial disease. Good seed will sink to the bottom. Don't ferment too long or the seed may start to germinate. Wash it clean and dry thoroughly.

Tomato is very easy seed to keep; I have heard of seed germinating from frozen tomatoes and dried tomatoes. We always get a good crop from the chook yard and spring compost.

Seeds are viable for 3 years.

To prevent seed-borne tomato diseases, tomato seed can be soaked overnight in garlic spray, or simply chop a garlic bulb up finely in a cup of water and pour this over the seed.

Turnip

Turnips readily cross, and you need a good kilometre between varieties to ensure they grow true-to-type. On the other hand, my foliage turnips have been reseeding themselves for years — if they have changed at all, it's for the better.

Turnips may also cross with rape, if you have a paddock of rape nearby, and sometimes with mustard, radish, Chinese cabbage or even the wild turnip weed. However, I have had all of these growing near my flowering turnips and have noticed that the bees seem to prefer only to go to one crop at a time. As I said, I don't appear to have had any cross-pollination.

I simply collect seed from the last turnips to go to seed in spring; when the seed heads are dry I cut them off and wrap them in newspaper, and plant next spring.

Seed is viable for 5 to 6 years.

Zucchini

Zucchinis need to become 'overmature', in terms of eating quality, before the seed is ripe. The fruit should be enormous, as large as it will grow, and starting to pale. The seeds inside will be large and tough.

Most zucchini seed sold is hybrid; it definitely doesn't come true-to-type if you keep it. I have tried several times and the results have all been bad, not even edible. Buy open-pollinated, non-hybrid seed if you want to keep your own seed.

Zucchini varieties cross-pollinate. Keep them separate or pick off the male flowers on one plant (the ones that don't have small zucchinis on them) until the female flowers on the other bush set fruit. Tie a loose band around that fruit so you know it has had the correct pollination.

Scrape zucchini seed out into a jar and ferment it for at least a week, stirring every day until the seed sinks to the bottom. Wash the seed and dry it in the sun.

Seed is viable for 5 to 10 years.

Seed from the supermarket

If you don't have a garden to harvest seed from, try the supermarket. Your range of varieties will be limited, but the seed will be fresh and much cheaper than that bought in packets.

Beans and lentils (dried)

These will only germinate if they are reasonably fresh, and haven't been irradiated. Choose fresh-looking lentils or dried beans, with no dust at the bottom of the packet, or signs of insect damage. Soak overnight and then plant them. I have done this with soy beans, chick peas, lima beans, red kidney beans and green and brown lentils. It doesn't work with dried peas, though, as these may be partly cooked before they are dried.

Beans and peas (fresh)

If the peas in each pod are large and swollen, the seed is probably ripe enough to germinate. I have had more luck with peas than beans; beans are usually picked too young for the seed to be really ripe (peas should be too, but aren't). Plant at once, or dry them to keep.

Beetroot

Plant the whole beetroot, leaf end up and pointy bit down. If it isn't too old it may start to shoot again and go to seed.

Broad bean

Large, fat broad beans may be ripe enough for seed. Make sure the seed is fully formed inside.

Cabbage

Plant the cabbage in spring, as long as it has some stalk left and it hasn't rotted. Take off the bottom third leaves first, to make the stalk longer, and plant it up to the next lot of leaves. Pack the soil around it firmly. I get about a 50 per cent success rate — the other half rots. Keep the plants in semi-shade so that they don't dry out in hot sunlight. Remember that they don't have roots to feed them, and must be kept moist. Stake them when they start to shoot.

Canary seed

Canary seed will give you millet — small fine seeds that can be added to stews or bread, or fed to the canary. Sow in spring through summer.

Capsicum

The seed of dark red capsicum, which is so ripe it seems thin skinned, can be dried and sown. Most capsicums in the shops, however, are still green. These can be left till they turn red, then the seed harvested. The riper the capsicum is though, the more chance there is that the seed is large and ripe enough to germinate.

Carrot

Your children may have done this: choose a dark, orange, thickish carrot and cut off the top in a piece about as long as your thumb. Place the piece on wet cotton wool and it should start to sprout. Plant this out in the garden so that just the top is showing. By the end of the season it should have gone to seed. Keep it staked so it doesn't fall over.

Alternatively, plant the whole carrot back in the garden and wait for it to shoot again. This will give you a better base for the seed head.

Choko

Choose the largest choko you can, preferably with the seed just starting to poke out the top. Leave it in a dry, dark, well-ventilated place until it starts to shoot. Plant it in spring with the shoot upward. If it is shooting strongly in mid-winter, plant it in a pot inside in a well-lit spot. Shooting can be slowed down in the refrigerator, or you can plant the choko in a pot in mid-winter, and keep it growing inside near a well-lit window till you are ready to plant it out in spring.

Corn

Very ripe corn (and this sometimes appears in supermarkets) which is too chewy to be tasty, can be dried, kept and sown as seed. Very ripe corn should have each kernel slightly separated. Beware though, as it is almost certainly hybrid and will not come true-to-type.

Cucumber

Most cucumbers aren't ripe enough to have mature seed to plant. If you do find one that is yellowing, however, you might try the seed from it. Germinate it on blotting paper or cotton wool first to test without wasting potting space.

Eggplant

Sometimes you find an eggplant that is very dark, ripe and has dark seeds in it. These can be planted. Eggplant can also be left in the cupboard until it starts to wrinkle — the seed may ripen inside. If you want to collect seed, choose the largest, darkest eggplant in the store.

Jerusalem artichoke

Plant artichokes once and you'll always have them. Choose the fattest tubers you can. Keep them in a dark, dry place (not the refrigerator) and plant in spring, or leave them in a temporary pot on the windowsill if they start to shrivel during winter.

Kumera

Kumeras are New Zealand sweet potatoes, not real sweet potatoes. They are more cold tolerant. Choose fat tubers. Plant after the frosts are over and keep weed-free.

Leek

If leeks have enough of their roots left (and many have), soak them in water overnight and plant deeply, hilling up round the sides and staking to keep the plant stable. The leek should start to grow again and will go to seed very quickly.

Melon and pumpkin

The riper the melon or pumpkin, the more likely it is that the seed will germinate. (You can tell if a melon is ripe by looking at its shape — melons should be evenly round, not bulging at one end. Pale streaks or white seeds may also mean that it has been picked too soon. The stems should also come clean off the fruit when it's ripe.) Unfortunately, most really ripe melons and pumpkins come mid- or late season — the early ones are rarely ripe enough — so that when you do get the seed it is too late to plant it. Dry it for next year. Melon and pumpkin seed should be hard shelled when it is ripe (unless it is pepita or triple-treat pumpkin seed which does not have a hull).

Mushroom

Mushroom spores are the small black specks that fall out of the underside (gills) of mature mushrooms. Make sure the mushrooms are kept dry, at room temperature, or they may rot before shedding spores. Leave the mushrooms on a piece of white paper, which will show the spores when they fall out. Then place the mushrooms in a paper bag to collect the spores. Store the spores in a paper bag, in a dry place.
In their natural state, mushrooms come up in autumn, in shady, moist areas. However, inside you can grow them year round. Press the spores into moist compost, and keep this in a warm, darkish place: near the stove or the hot water service is perfect.

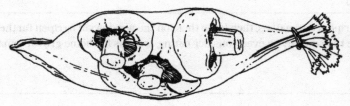

Onion

Take a healthy looking onion, not squishy in the centre, and plant it so that the pointed side is upwards, just poking out of the soil. Wait. Two times out of three it will start to sprout again (if it hasn't been artificially treated to stop sprouting). These sprouts will eventually go to seed; and the seed can be harvested.

Parsnip

See Carrot

Potato

Technically, it is illegal in most states to grow potatoes from any but certified seed. Don't grow non-certified seed in a potato growing area — you may spread disease. Aphids can carry potato virus for many kilometres, and it is unfair to growers. Choose healthy looking potatoes; avoid ones with long shoots as these may be infected with a virus.

Choosing your seed potatoes from the supermarket also gives you access to gourmet varieties, most of which aren't sold in garden centres as seed potatoes and have to be ordered in bulk (even then they are hard to get hold of). Look for waxy yellow potatoes, or white-fleshed perfect baking colibans.

Radish

Radishes can be planted again, up to their necks in soil. They should start to shoot quite quickly and this shoot will form a seed head.

Sunflower

Choose a fresh looking packet of cockle seed. Plant from spring through summer.

Sweet potato

Choose tubers that have started to sprout — many sweet potatoes are chemically treated to stop sprouting. Buy organic potatoes if you can.

Tomato

Choose ripe red tomatoes, then leave them on the windowsill to ripen further. When they are too squashy to even consider eating, treat as for home-grown tomatoes.

Turnip

See Carrot

4 Fruit

Fruit carries the seed of most plants. With the exception of a few species like bananas and strawberries, if you have the fruit you have enough genetic material to grow more fruit.

Many seedling trees, however, don't breed true-to-type, either because their parents were hybrids or because two varieties naturally crossed. While this is of concern to commercial growers who need all their fruit to look the same for marketing purposes (and to be all at the same stage at the same time for spraying and picking), it needn't concern the home grower. I have grown hundreds of seedling trees (about 170 different sorts), and most have been very like their parents — in many cases indistinguishable. (Sadly — I keep hoping I'll find a new variety!) Even when they weren't, all bore good fruit. I find, in fact, that it is the ones that vary slightly from their parents that I prize most: in some cases because they are better adapted and in other cases simply because they provide slightly different fruit from any I can buy.

It's very easy to grow fruit from seed; it's cheap (free in fact); and you end up with much hardier plants, as long as you don't keep any plants that don't flourish. If, after several years, you find you don't like the fruit the plants produce, graft or bud one or several named varieties onto them.

Grafted plants DON'T necessarily produce fruit faster! The act of grafting really stresses a tree — and the place where the two grafts meet will always be weaker than the rest of the tree, and is where disease or pests may enter. (Wooly aphids, for example, often start their infestation at the graft point.)

A grafted tree will usually give you a LITTLE fruit before a seedling will. But the seedling will usually grow faster than the grafted tree, and so give you MORE fruit sooner.

The faster a tree grows, too, the bigger its root stock will be; and the bigger the roots are, the more drought, heat, cold and wind resistant it will be. Seedlings are often much hardier!

There is another aspect too. Many fruit trees are grown on semi-dwarfing stock, to keep them neat for orchards and backyards. Semi-dwarfing stock is 'semi-dwarfing' because it's less vigorous — it simply doesn't grow as fast.

If you want a big root system FAST so your tree can withstand droughts, grow your own!

Very, very rarely a seedling tree will take much longer to bear than a grafted one. I've found a seedling loquat that took ten years to bear, and a seedling chestnut that took eight years, compared to the grafted ones which took five years. But apart from those, the seedlings have won every time.

PS. One real exception is passionfruit. Grafted passionfruit are always more vigorous, as they are grafted onto very vigorous stock. They are more heat, cold, and drought resistant, and far less prone to disease. I HAVE grown seedling passionfruit, but really recommend grafted ones.

Preparing seed

The seed of most evergreen fruit trees, like citrus, can usually be planted straight away, or kept till needed once the pulp around it is removed.

Deciduous trees can be more complicated. You can plant the seed straight from the fruit, but it may take a while to germinate. Most deciduous seed is available in summer or autumn, and it will probably (but not always) need winter chilling before it will germinate.

Otherwise, take the dried deciduous seed, dip it in hot water for 10 seconds, take it out for 30 seconds, and dip again. Now place it in moist pots in the refrigerator for about 2 months. Check for germination each day after the first month, and plant out as it is ready.

Don't keep seed from deciduous trees in a warm cupboard over winter and expect it to germinate in spring. It won't have been chilled — especially if your house is heated. Keep the seed in the refrigerator until spring or outside so its gets cold.

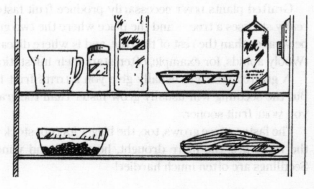

If deciduous seed fails to germinate just after picking, keep it in the refrigerator in moist soil for about 2 months.

If you want to try germinating fresh seed, drop it in warm water straight from the fruit, soak it for 2 days, then place it in a pot in a plastic bag or under a glass jar on a warm windowsill. It should germinate in 2 weeks. If it doesn't, you'll have to wait till spring.

Growing your own fruit

Almond (*Prunus dulcis*)

Almonds need some chilling, a well-drained soil and freedom from late spring frost. Sow the fresh seed where the tree is to grow. Graft onto the growing seedling, if you decide to graft.

Apple (*Malus sylvestris*)

Many apples need winter chilling before they bear. Anna, Tropic Apple, Granny Smith, Lady Williams, Gravenstein and Delicious apples need less chilling. I've grown eight seedling apples (so far). All fruited well, and fast.

Apple trees can be grown from seed, by layering, sometimes by tip cuttings, but most apples are grafted or budded onto seedlings. Northern Spy is the most popular rootstock as it is resistant to woolly aphid and tolerates drought. Apples may be grafted onto dwarfing rootstocks for small or medium trees.

You can also take root cuttings of apples, though this will only give you the root-stock variety which is likely to be Northern Spy. Take cuttings of the main roots, close to the stem, in winter. Make sure there is some main root and some smaller roots; and make sure you don't plant the root upside down. The root cutting should grow extremely quickly once it starts to shoot in spring.

Apricot (*Prunus armeniaca*)

Apricots need sun, well-drained soil, as little pruning as possible, and freedom from late spring frosts.

Apricot trees can be grown from seed or by layering. Apricots from seed are close enough to true-to-type for the home gardener, but not for commercial production. Trees grown on site do much better than those that have been transplanted.

Graft apricots onto peach, apricot or plum stock. Peach stock produces a smaller tree; plum stock produces large, heavy-bearing trees; and apricot stock is suitable except in wet areas.

Avocado (*Persea gratissirna*)

Avocado seedlings grow very quickly, straight and tall. They won't bear till they are about 4 metres tall — and by then you may think they will never bear. But, suddenly, the next year, you'll see them covered in blossom, then laden with fruit. I've grown about 70 seedlings so far. All fruit superbly. Avocados need a well-drained, moist, fertile soil, and wind protection. They will tolerate only light frost. Propagation is by seed, cuttings, or layering.

When planting seed, don't cover it entirely — the shoot appears between the two halves. Some people get avocados to shoot by wedging them between two toothpicks in a glass of water; others find young trees springing up in their compost.

Plant avocado seeds with the pointy end downwards, leaving half the stone out of the soil. Cover the pot with plastic or cover the seed with an inverted glass jar. Keep in indirect light. The seed will split as the shoot develops. Take the plastic off after the first two leaves appear.

Avocado seeds sprout leaves
from the blunt end of the seed.
Always plant seeds point
downwards.

Seeding avocados aren't supposed to grow true-to-type and should be grafted for commercial orchards. But perhaps commercial avocados now come from such a limited gene pool that there are fewer variations than there used to be.

Avocados can also be propagated by softwood cuttings in late summer to early autumn, hardwood cuttings in late winter to spring, and by layering. Protect young trees from frost and full sun (I use hessian covers) and make sure the soil is moist.

Banana

Bananas need moist, fertile, well-drained soil, and tolerate only light frost. Wild bananas reproduce by seed (those black spots in the centre of the fruit are the remnants of proper seeds), but cultivated varieties don't. Cut and plant the suckers in spring. Remove the top part, so only the fleshy base is used for planting.

Berries

Berries are a cool to temperate climate crop, apart from specially bred subtropical strawberry varieties.

Raspberries are usually grown by transplanting suckers in winter; any root damage will increase the tendency for plants to sucker.

Brambleberries, such as thornless blackberries, marionberries and loganberries, are usually propagated by tip layering. The growing top of a new cane is buried in late summer; then cut off from the parent plant in winter, and transplanted in spring.

Blueberries need an acidic, well-drained, moist, fertile soil. The berries taste best if grown in a cold climate. Plant the fruit when it is fully ripe (dark purple), or dry the seeds. Seedlings don't come true-to-type and may vary a lot.

Hardwood cuttings take easily in late winter to early spring. Softwood cuttings may take in summer to autumn, but usually need high humidity by keeping them under plastic or glass, or by using a mist sprayer.

Strawberries are usually grown from runners planted in February, though, if kept moist and mulched, they can be planted at any time. Some strawberry varieties and old-fashioned alpine strawberries can be grown from seed.

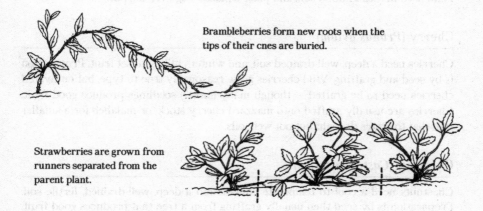

Brambleberries form new roots when the tips of their cnes are buried.

Strawberries are grown from runners separated from the parent plant.

Brazil nut (*Bertholletia excelsa*)

Brazil nuts needs a hot, moist climate. Propagation is by seed — a warm, moist soil is necessary for germination.

Breadfruit tree (*Artocarpus communis*)

The breadfruit tree needs subtropical to tropical conditions, and a deep, moist, well-drained, humus-rich soil. Propagation is by softwood cuttings grown in a glasshouse.

Cape gooseberry (*Physalis peruviania*)

Cape gooseberry needs a position in full sun or semi-shade in a moist soil. It will tolerate light frost. Seed grows easily. Plant either the whole ripe fruit or separate the seed as with tomato. Don't cover the seed with soil when you plant it though, and put plastic or glass over the pot.

Cape gooseberries also take from cuttings; use old wood and strike it in damp sand. (Seedlings, however, are more reliable than cuttings.) Tip layering can also be successful; bury a new shoot in summer with only the tip exposed. Cut the shoot free of its parent in winter and transplant it in spring.

Carob (*Ceratonia siliqua*)

The carob tree needs full sun and a well-drained soil. It tolerates frost, heat and drought. Seeds should germinate within a month of planting. Dried seeds may be soaked first to speed up germination. You need a male and female plant for pollination, so you may need to grow a few trees to be sure, or graft from trees you know to be male or female.

Cashew (*Anacardium occidentale*)

Cashews grow in a subtropical to tropical climate in deep, well-drained, moist soil. Plant seed in moist humid soil, and place a plastic bag over the pot.

Cherry (*Prunus avium*)

Cherries need a deep, well-drained soil, and winter chilling to set fruit. Propagation is by seed and grafting. Wild cherries grow reasonably true-to-type, but cultivated cherries need to be grafted – though many (most?) seedlings produce good fruit. Cherries are usually grafted onto mazzard cherry stock, or malaheb for a smaller tree that tolerates drought but not wet soils.

Chestnut (*Castanea sativa*)

Chestnuts need a cool to temperate climate and a deep, well-drained, fertile soil. Propagation is by seed then usually grafting from a tree that produces good fruit. There is better germination after stratification, so treat as deciduous tree seed.

Don't bother planting seed unless the nuts are good and fat. It's best to only plant from a tree you know to be an excellent bearer.

Citrus

Citrus plants tolerate light frost only, needing full sun and a deep, well-drained soil with adequate moisture in summer. Plants are usually grown from seed, then grafted, or from cuttings. Mandarins can be layered.

I've found seedling citrus MUCH more cold and drought hardy, and good bearers. But we have well drained soil. In wetter areas, or with soils high in clay, you may find that you need to graft your citrus onto rootstocks that are resistant to root rots.

Citrus cuttings

Take new growth, about 20 cm long, and make the cut just below a bud. Dip the end in rooting powder, then set it in clean sand and keep moist, covered with plastic. Place it in a shady spot at about 25° to 30°C. Only about 10 per cent (or less) of cuttings take. In warm weather, cuttings will start to root in about 2 months; autumn cuttings may survive and stay green but not make roots till spring. Don't discard any cutting until it turns brown. Lemon and orange cuttings appear to be the most successful – mandarin rarely takes. Air layering is best for mandarin and may also have some success with oranges.

Grafted citrus

Rough lemon used to be the most common rootstock, but is susceptible to collar rot. Citrange is probably a better choice nowadays, though it may be hard to get hold of for the home grower. Citrus can be grafted onto orange seedlings for a small tree – though orange also is susceptible to collar rot. Try to keep mulch and long grass away from the trunk.

If you decide to grow a lot of citrus, it may be worthwhile to grow a citrus root-stock like bush lemon or citrange just to get fruit for seeds to use as rootstock.

Citrus seedlings usually start to fruit after about 2-6 years, depending on climate, about the same age as grafted trees will take to bear in the same climate.

Native citrus: these grow from seeds or cuttings, as above.

Coconut (*Cocos nucifera*)

Coconut can be grown indoors, but needs full sun, and a minimum temperature of 20°C. Coconuts for germination should be full of milk — shake them first to check. Wash the coconut and place it in a polythene bag, still wet, and hang it in the sunlight. Remove the coconut when it is covered in short, white roots. Plant in moist but well-drained soil.

Cornelian cherry (*Corus mas*)

This tree is hardy in a wide range of conditions, though it needs a cold climate. Propagation is by seed or cuttings, either softwood or hardwood.

Currant (*Ribes* sp.)

Currants need a cool climate and fertile, moist soil. Take hardwood cuttings of the current season's growth, about 20 to 30 cm long. Cut just below a bud. Plant into moist soil in a semi-shaded position, leaving a couple of buds above ground and several below. The cutting should shoot in spring.

Date (*Phoenix dactylifera*)

Dates need full sun, low humidity, and a frost-free position. You need male and female trees, so you need to plant a few. You can germinate the seed of either fresh or dried dates, though dried seed germinates faster. Soak the seed for 3 days in warm water, changing the water every day. Sow the seed about 2 cm deep in well-drained soil. Germination may take 1 to 8 months. Do not detach the seed from the young plant when you transplant it.

Feijoa or pineapple guava (*Feijoa sellowiana*)

Feijoas tolerate a wide range of conditions, though prefer a frost-free, well-drained site. Collect seed from autumn fruit and treat as for tomato. Seedlings take about 5 years to fruit. Hardwood cuttings can be taken in winter; buried deeply in sand and covered with an inverted glass jar. Softwood cuttings can be taken in mid-summer. Note that you usually need two feijoa trees to get fruit.

Fig (*Ficus carica*)

Figs need a sunny position and well-drained soil; they tolerate heat and moderate frost. Fig trees grow very easily and quickly from cuttings. Take pieces, about 20 cm long, from mature wood (that can be snapped), just below a bud. Plant them to a depth of about a third of their length in a mix of half sand and half soil. Let the cuttings dry out before planting so that they don't rot. Keep the cuttings in semi-shade.

   Fig trees also grow from suckers. These should be dug out in winter using a sharp spade, though, if kept moist, suckers can be taken at any time of the year in cool or rainy weather.

Gooseberries (*Ribes* sp.)

Gooseberries need a cool to temperate climate. You can use cuttings or seed. Take cuttings of 1-year-old wood in late winter to early spring, and plant in sandy soil. Seed may be planted, either fresh or dry, but cuttings give a quicker result.

Grapes

The needs of grapes vary with the variety. Cuttings are the usual method of propagation, and strike very easily. Layering often works; and is quicker than cuttings. Some varieties grow from seed, but seedlings take much longer to grow than cuttings.

   Cuttings, about 90 cm long, pencil-thick, are taken in late winter to early spring. Cut off all buds except the top two. In many areas grapes should be grafted onto phylloxera-resistant rootstocks, so ask your horticultural adviser or local Department of Rural Affairs for advice.

Guava (*Psidiurn guajava*)

Guava tolerates light frost, high temperatures and drought. Place fresh or dried seed on top of the soil; cover the pot with plastic wrap or an inverted glass jar. The seeds should germinate in a month. Take cuttings from new growth. Remove the leaves without harming the leaf buds, and plant the cutting deep enough so that at least three buds are covered. Keep in the shade or semi-shade at about 20-25°C. New growth should appear in 1 or 2 months. Rooting powder increases the chance of success. Cuttings must be in moist, well-drained soil or they will rot or fail to root. Guavas can also be air layered or grafted.

Hazelnut, filbert (*Corylus avellana*)

The hazelnut prefers deep, well-drained soil. Preparation can be by seed (though offspring are not true-to-type), but is usually by suckers or grafting onto suckers, or by tip layering. There are a lot of poor quality seedlings around — only propagate from a tree that bears lots of good quality fruit. You'll need two compatible varieties, too, for good pollination.

Kiwi fruit

Kiwi fruit must have a well-drained, moist soil. Plants will only tolerate light frost, so grow them next to a building in cold climates. To obtain seed, place slices of ripe fruit in warm water and leave for a few days until the seed separates. Dry the seed and place it on top of soil in a pot (don't cover it). Cover the pot with plastic wrap, a plastic bag, or a glass jar. Watering can dislodge tiny roots. Seed should germinate within 2 weeks in warm conditions.

Kiwi fruit need male and female plants in order to set fruit, so you may need to plant several seedlings to be sure. Alternatively you can graft from a known plant onto a seedling.

Kiwi fruit cuttings are taken in mid-winter. They should be hardwood, about 45 cm long, and planted to half their length in sandy soil. Keep them moist.

Kiwi fruit can also be grown from root cuttings. Dig up the roots in early winter, and cut them into pieces about as long as your hand and as wide as a pencil, with some stringy roots attached. These cuttings should all grow.

Lilly pilly (*Eugenia* and *Syzigium* spp.)

These all grow fairly true-to-type from seed, though it depends how much natural variation there is where the seeds came from — the more the parents may vary, the more chance there is that you'll get variations in the offspring. If find all lilly pilly survive frost in a sheltered garden, even ones from Cape York — but they DO need shelter from other trees. Seedlings grow so fast, and fruit so well, that I've never tried any other form of propagation. But they can also be grafted.

Loquat (*Eriobotrya japonica*)

The loquat tolerates light frost and heat. Seed germinates easily, either fresh or dried. Although trees don't come true-to-type and seedlings may take longer to fruit (up to 15 years), seed is still adequate for the home gardener. Pick the fruit for seed when it is fully ripe and soft.

Loquats can also be air layered or grafted onto quince stock.

Lychee (*Litchi chinensis*)

Lychees need well-drained, acid soil, rich in humus. They tolerate only mild frosts.

As seedlings grow slowly and don't fruit for up to 10 years, propagation by air layering or grafting is more common. Seed is sown fresh from the fruit, about 1 cm deep, in a humus-rich soil. It should be placed in a semi-shaded, warm position and kept moist. The fresher the fruit, the sooner the seed will germinate. This usually takes about a month.

Cuttings should be woody, as tip cuttings rot.

Macadamia (*Macadamia* sp.)

Macadamias tolerate only light frost, needing deep, moist, well-drained soil. Tetraphylla macadamias, which have very VERY hard shelled nuts, will take light frosts, or heavy frosts in a sheltered garden. Macadamias grow from seed, though commercial plantings are usually grafted to get early fruiting and ensure large nuts. Cuttings are rarely successful.

Mango (*Mangifera indica*)

Mangoes like a hot climate, and only tolerate light frost when established. They need a moist, fertile, deep, well-drained soil.

Propagation is by seed then grafting onto seedlings. Plant the seed with the round end down and the tip just under the soil. Keep warm and shaded; the young shoots are even more vulnerable to frost than mango trees. Seed sown under a glass jar or plastic bag will germinate faster.

If your mango wasn't fully ripe (it should be squashy yellow and very soft), you will need to cut open the seed before planting, as the shell may be too tough. Cut the seed at the pointed end with a sharp knife for a few centimetres, then twist the seed with both hands till you can stick your finger into the slit.

Two shoots come out of each mango seed. Cut off the smaller one.

Mulberries

Black mulberry (*Morus nigra*) tolerates heat and frost, and needs a deep, well-drained soil. Propagation is by seed, cutting, layering or grafting. Take finger-thick cuttings in spring, and plant them so that at least two buds are under the soil. Grow them in semi-shade until they are well-established.

White mulberry (*Morus alba*) also tolerates heat and frost, needing a deep, well-drained soil. Propagation is by seed or spring cuttings, though usually by grafting onto seedlings. Cuttings need a cool soil and sunlight.

Olive (*Olea europaea*)

Olives tolerate heat and mild frost, needing full sun and a well-drained soil. Propagation is by cuttings, shoots or suckers. Seedlings don't grow true-to-type. Germination can be very slow, and the resulting trees may not fruit for many years or may not fruit at all. (On the other hand, my seedling olives fruited at the same time as my grafted plants, and have proved hardy and fast-growing.)

Seeds should be fresh. Choose a black olive and rub the flesh off first. Germination should be within a month, though older seed may take up to 4 months to germinate.

Take olive cuttings, about 20 cm long, in spring and plant them to half their depth in wet sand. Cover with plastic or a glass bottle and keep moist in the semi-shade. They should root in about 2 months.

Passionfruit (*Passiflora edulis*)

Passionfruit tolerates mild frost only. It needs a well-drained soil and a sunny position, though in hotter areas it needs semi-shade. Passionfruit is one plant that really does far better when grafted onto a vigorous rootstock. (The rootstock won't produce good fruit.)

Passionfruit grows from seed or cuttings. Choose a ripe, wrinkled, black passionfruit, and soak the seed in warm water to clean off the flesh. Sow the seed fresh or dry in spring in a humus-rich soil; don't cover the seed with soil. Cover the pot with a plastic bag or an inverted glass jar and keep in the semi-shade. The seed should germinate in 2 to 3 weeks at 25°C.

Cuttings of semi-matured shoots, about 20 cm long, can be taken in early or late summer just below a leaf axil. Dip in root powder before planting for best results. Plant in peat or damp humus-rich sterilised soil. (Cuttings are very prone to rotting, so sterilised soil must be used.) Keep in semi-shade, preferably at around 20°C. Cuttings should start to root in 3 weeks, but don't throw any out until they turn brown.

Pawpaw (*Carica papaya*)

Pawpaw prefers full sun and high humidity. Soil should be moist, but well-drained, and the position frost-free.

Propagation is by seed, which germinates easily, or by hardwood cuttings.

Pawpaw seed only germinates if there are male and female trees around; females will sometimes bear fruit without males. When you plant the seed, make sure the soil is well-drained. Seed germinates in 1 to 2 weeks and keeps for 3 to 5 years.

Because of the shape of the pawpaw tree, taking a cutting usually means taking the top of the tree. Let it dry out before planting so it doesn't rot; cover the cut on the tree where it was taken, so the wood doesn't rot. Plant in sterilised soil.

Peach (*Prunus persica*)

All peaches need winter chilling, though some varieties need more chilling than others. They also need a well-drained soil and freedom from late spring frost.

Propagation is by grafting onto seedlings. Most peach seedlings I've known have fruited. A couple of times the fruit has been smaller than the parent, even under good cultivation. Wild peach seedlings may not fruit at all, though this may be because they haven't been pruned, as peaches fruit on 1-year-old wood. But I've never known any peach seedling not to fruit — and most I've known have fruited, year after year, and without pruning too.

Graft peaches onto apricot, almond, plum or peach seedling stock. Plum stock is tolerant of wet areas, but can harbour a virus that weakens the graft after a few years (I once had a whole nursery batch, some 45 trees, die for this reason). Plum stock produces a smaller tree than peach stock.

Peach cuttings, either winter hardwood or spring softwood, take from some varieties.

Peanut (*Arachis hypogaea*)

Peanuts need full sun and 6 frost-free months with a night temperature not below 15°C and preferably around 20°C. Thick mulch means you can grow them at lower night temperatures, but high daytime temperatures, say 20 to 25°C, are essential or they won't ripen. Choose fresh peanuts in their shells; shell them or plant in the shell. Plant peanuts when the temperature is around 20°C — in cold areas you can start them on a warm windowsill.

Fresh peanuts (not roasted) are really peanut seeds.

Pear (*Prunus comrnunis*)

You need two pear varieties for good pollination, though often a single pear can fruit well. However, it may not produce viable seed — seed which will grow into a tree — if it hasn't been pollinated, and the seeds or core may look malformed. Pears are generally propagated by grafting onto seedlings. Pear seedlings vary, though many (most?) come true-to-type.

Pears are usually grafted onto wild pear stock or onto quince stock for a smaller tree. Pear or quince stock produce earlier fruit which matures faster, but quince stock isn't suitable for wet areas. Some pear varieties aren't compatible with quince stock.

Pear cuttings sometimes take, depending on the variety.

Pecan (*Carya illinoiensis*)

Pecan nuts grow well in a mild, humid climate with hot summers. They need a deep, well-drained fertile soil.

Pecans are propagated by seed. The taproot grows quickly and is very long. This makes seedlings hard to transplant; they die if the root is broken. You need to use long pots, like old milk cartons, and transplant the seedlings by cutting out the bottom of the pot. Theoretically you need two or more varieties for nut production. However, I've grown one pecan for 20 years, and it's borne happily by itself for the past 15 years. Commercial trees are usually budded or grafted onto seedlings.

Persimmon (*Diospyros kaki*)

Persimmons will tolerate moderate frosts as well as subtropical heat. Most commercial fruit is seedless; old-fashioned varieties have seeds and these can be planted after chilling, but may not be fertile. They probably will be, though. You can then graft on wood from the newer varieties, which are sweeter and less mushy.

Pineapple (*Ananas comosus*)

Pineapple needs a frost-free spot (or be subject to only light frosts in winter), full sun, and temperatures of 25 to 30°C to mature.

Take the top off a pineapple, and strip off the bottom third of the leaves until you can see rows of brown spots. Plant the top so that these are covered — the roots develop from them — though let the pineapple dry for 3 days before planting. In cold areas plant into a pot and cover with a plastic bag, and keep on a warm patio or windowsill for a year or two, until the plant is well-established. Pineapples fruit in 3 years in warm climates, but may take much longer in cold areas.

Pistachio (*Pistacia vera*)

Pistachios need a well-drained soil, in a position sheltered from strong wind, and will tolerate light frost. Although they will grow in cold climates, pistachios will only fruit reliably in milder climates. But you may also find in cold climates that your pistachio will bear after looking mature and fruitless for several years. Like many warm climate trees they seem to need a long breathing space to acclimatise. One male plant is needed to pollinate five to six female plants.

Don't try to plant a roasted, salted pistachio. Soak raw pistachios in warm water for 3 days, then plant them half-covered with soil. Don't cover with plastic or the seed may rot. Germination should take about a month. Pistachios grow reasonably true-to-type, but should be grafted for commercial orchards (usually grafted onto *Pistacia terebinthus*) to hasten bearing.

PS. Fresh pistachios, straight from the tree, don't need roasting and salting for flavour — they are delicious.

Plum (*Prunus domestica*)

Most plum seedlings will produce good fruit. Some may not fruit at all, though I've never known one that didn't. Japanese plums don't need a pollinator; European plums do. Propagation is generally by grafting onto seedlings.

Plum, peach, almond, and apricot rootstocks can be used for grafting, though cherry plum is the most common. Peach and privet stock can be used in light soils; they produce smaller, though good-bearing trees.

Pomegranate (*Punica granatum*)

Pomegranate is frost, heat, and drought tolerant, once established. It needs sun and shelter from harsh wind. Propagation is by seed, suckers, layering or cuttings. Seed can be planted fresh or dried. Cuttings, about 20 cm long, should be taken in spring, and planted to half their length in sandy soil. Keep them at about 20 to 30°C, and new growth should appear in 1 to 2 months.

Quince (*Cydonia oblonga*)

Quince is both frost and heat tolerant. Propagation is by cuttings or root division, then grafting; or by suckers. Trees sucker easily and these may be uprooted and replanted. You can also plant the seeds.

Tamarillo (*Cyphomandra* sp.)

Tamarillos tolerate only very light frost and need well-drained, fertile soil. Tamarillos grown from seed are fairly true-to-type if only one variety has been grown, and bear in about 2 years. If more than one variety has been grown you get the usual lucky dip to see which parent's characteristics are inherited. Seeds can take up to six months to germinate, but can also germinate in about three weeks. Plants can also be grown from cuttings of 1-year-old wood, or from layering. Our tamarillo trees layer naturally. As the old branches break down and spread across the soil, more roots form along them in the mulch around the trees.

Walnut (*luglans* sp.)

Walnuts tolerate moderate frost, and need deep, moist, well-drained fertile soil. Propagation is by seed or grafting onto seedlings.

An orchard from the supermarket shelves

Specialist fruit sections are an excellent way to find seed of rare or new varieties, and a cheap source of other seed. Our first tamarillos grew from the supermarket; so did our chokos, one of our oranges, mandarins, apricots, some of our plums, one of our apple trees, several new varieties of avocado, and a host of other plants. Look for banana passionfruit, ordinary passionfruit, tamarillos, fresh lychees or unusual varieties of avocado — they may not come quite true-to-type but will probably be close.

Apples won't grow true-to-type, but will probably resemble their parents, particularly as most orchards only have one or two varieties. Choose only very ripe apples, and if the seeds and core seem malformed, don't bother as they may not have been pollinated.

Nashi or oriental pear grown from seed will not be true-to-type, but will probably resemble the parents. Persimmon seeds won't be fertile unless cross-pollinated, though commercial persimmons are more likely to be fertile than home-grown fruit.

Look for cherries, citrus (limes, blood oranges or pink-fleshed grapefruit) and plums (Japanese plums are reasonably true-to-type, but European plums vary). Plant your apricot stones, pineapple tops, kiwi fruit seeds, peach pips, almonds and all other nuts, as long as they are fresh (not roasted), as well as blueberries, feijoas and pepinos.

With very few exceptions (like strawberries and bananas), most fruit contains seed, and this can be planted. As long as you realise you may not get an identical copy of the parent fruit, seed from commercial fruit orchards almost always produces worthwhile offspring.

5 Flowers and Other Ornamentals

The classic cottage garden grew from bits from someone else's garden — not from plants bought at a garden centre. There is no reason why gardens today can't be the same. Flowers may be more showy than fruit or vegies, but they are no more difficult to reproduce. And nearly always it's very, very easy to grow them from seeds or cuttings.

Ornamental shrubs and trees are expensive to buy, usually because they are big and take up space, and space costs a lot if you run a nursery or have to transport plants. With very few exceptions, though, ornamental trees and shrubs are easy to grow — after all, they were all once wild forest species, growing by themselves, without any human aid at all. Most of the popular plants also grow quickly.

The backbone of our garden was created with cuttings from Jean Hobbins' garden down the road. They're all an example of what you can grow by just taking a bit of wood from another plant and, literally, pushing it in where you want it to grow. (A note, though: the ground should be fairly moist and well-drained; cuttings won't take in pure clay or shale.) Some of the plants that Jean gave us as seeds or cuttings include: carnations, daisies (marguerites, shasta daisies, etc), dianthus, elderberry, euryops, geraniums, lad's love, lavender, mints, old-fashioned rambling roses (cuttings never seem to fail and grow quickly), santolina, soapwort, tansy, wormwood, almost any bulb, tuber or rhizome — we harvested irises, ginger lilies, cannas, calla lilies, chrysanthemums and dahlias from our neighbours.

So how do you get a free 'seeds and cuttings' garden?

Ask you friends for cuttings or seeds. Mooch around your suburb or neighbourhood and ask gardeners for a bit of what you fancy. (Dedicated gardeners are usually both proud of their plants, and generous with cuttings.) Go to Open Garden Scheme gardens — but DO ASK FIRST before you take seeds or cuttings, as shrubs can be killed if too many visitors take freebies.

Join a garden club — most have 'sale tables' where members' plants are sold or swapped.

Look for seedling shrubs and trees under old plants — such as along streets. (They'll be dug up, mowed or poisoned if they are left, so dig them up and save them.) In old gardens, ask the owner if you can look among the leaf mould under the trees for seedlings.

Most ornamentals shed enormous amounts of seed, far more than you'll need. Keep an eye on your favourite trees to see when the seed is ripe and starts to fall. Stick some in your pocket as you pass. Even if you don't know the name of a tree you like, don't be put off. You'll almost certainly be able to grow it from seed, and as for its growing requirements, you need just give it roughly the same conditions as its parent and it'll be fine.

Never accept the myth that ornamental plants are the prerogative of nurseries and professional propagators — they're not. Ornamentals, like all other plants, belong to anyone who loves them.

Warning: ANY ornamental that grows too well can become a dangerous weed, especially near bushland. Around here, *grevillea rosmarifolia* has become a weed, and Cootamundra wattle, and red hot pokers. A friend in Wee Jasper has a problem with weedy agapanthus (it's too shady here in the valley for ours to go wild). Different areas will have different weed problems, and what may be safe — or dangerous — in one area, may be quite the opposite in another.

KEEP AN EYE ON YOUR GARDEN! If a plant starts spreading, hoick it out!

Remember, too, that plants may only produce viable seed after they've been growing for ten or even twenty years. I've seen supposedly sterile bridal broom produce seedlings after 14 years of doing what it was supposed to, that is, producing no viable seed at all. I'm VERY wary of imported ornamental grasses. Most are only trialled for a few years before they are declared safe for Australian gardens — and that isn't nearly long enough to really test their weed potential.

Departments of Agriculture in each state maintain websites with lists of weeds. But you too need to watch ALL new plants closely as well.

Annual flowers

Annual flowers — ones that are planted, flower, and die in the same year — are usually grown from seed. Collect the seed when the flower dies and keep it for next year. Try to take seed from early as well as late flowering plants, and any that seem to be particularly beautiful or hardy.

Like herbs and vegetables, if you grow two varieties of flowers together, say pink and white perennial peas, seed may not be true-to-type. If you want to preserve a colour or some other characteristic, use the methods for hand pollination described for vegetables. Some colours in particular seem to thrive at the expense of others, and you may need to do a little extra work to preserve the others.

Collecting seed from annual flowers

This is simple. Wait until the flowers are dying, then either tie a paper bag around them to catch the seed, or pull them out by the roots, tie them up in a sheltered spot (like a shed or verandah) with a paper bag round the flower and collect the seed later. Unlike vegetables you may want to collect the seed from the first plant to flower, rather than the last, or over a good selection of flowering times. As with vegetables, after a few years of selection you will get flowers that are well adapted to your conditions.

Perennial and biennial flowers

Biennials live for 2 years and perennials live indefinitely. Some perennials die down in winter (herbaceous perennials), while others stay green for the whole year.

Herbaceous perennials usually form large clumps. These can be divided every year, examples are achilleas, agapanthus, alstroemerias, astilbe, campanula, canna, chrysanthemum, clivia, eucomis, gazania, gerbera, helleborus (winter rose), Japanese anemone, perennial phlox, pyrethrum and salvias.

Nearly all perennials and biennials produce lots of seed, too, that can be collected.

Bulbs

Most bulbs are propagated by digging up and separating the new bulbs they make each year. They may, however, also set seed. Bulbs usually don't come true-to-type, though this is as good a reason as any for planting them, as all will be good, and some interesting, and some spectacular.

Agapanthus

Agapanthus tolerates light frost, and is a very adaptable plant. Collect the ripe seed in autumn. Agapanthus hybridise readily and you may find interesting seedlings. Otherwise divide clumps after flowering. Older plants are more likely to produce viable seed.

Warning: avoid agapanthus that produce lots of self-sown seedlings! These can, and do, become a major weed, especially near bushland. Another word for 'good survivor' is weed!

Belladonna lily (*Amaryllis belladonna*)

The belladonna lily is very adaptable, tolerating mild frost. Sow seed if any sets, or divide the tubers. Older bulbs are more likely to produce viable seed.

Canna lily

Canna lilies tolerate light frost. Dig up the rapidly-spreading rhizomes or roots in winter; cut into several pieces, each with at least one bud, and replant the pieces.

Cyclamen

Cyclamens need cool, shady conditions. They grow easily from seed and often seed themselves. Dig up the corms when the leaves die down and repot them.

Daffodil and jonquil (*Narcissus*)

Daffodils and jonquils are frost-hardy. They are usually propagated by dividing bulbs, though most set seed and this is often viable.

Dahlia

Dahlias are very tolerant. They can be grown from seed, tubers or cuttings. Collect the dead flower heads in autumn and dry them, then shake out the seed. Sow the seed in spring. It should germinate in 1 to 2 weeks.

Tubers can be separated in late winter or early spring, and replanted. You can also take dahlia cuttings. Take these from new growth in spring, with a bit of the last season's stalk. Cuttings without stalk will grow for one season, but probably won't produce a tuber, and reappear in the next year.

Warning: Tall, single dahlias grown from seed may become a weed, and wind-blown seedlings will come up everywhere. Avoid them near bushland.

Shake dead dahlia heads in autumn to collect the dahlia seed.

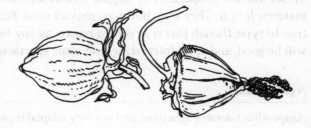

Ginger lily (*Hedychium*)

Hedychium tolerates only light frost and will do best in high humidity. Divide the rhizomes in early spring.

Kniphofia, red hot poker

These grow from division or seed. *Warning:* Avoid the big red varieties or pokers, as they can produce self-sown seedlings that soon become weeds, both in the garden and near bushland, especially in wet years. Older plants are more likely to produce viable seed.

Lilies (*Lilium*)

Needs vary according to species, though most lilies need a well-drained soil, cool conditions, shade around their bases and full sun on their flowers. All lilies grow easily from seed, which must be sown when very fresh. Lilies hybridise and seedlings may not be true-to-type. More accurate reproduction is by scaling the bulbs; do this as soon as you can after they flower. Lilies reproduce themselves naturally as the bulbs increase. Sometimes bulbs occur along the stem, and these can also be planted.

Warning: Avoid *Lilium longiflora* near bushland, especially in high rainfall areas, as it becomes a weed. ANY *Lilium* may become a weed near rainforest, wet or swampy areas.

Peruvian lily (*Alstroemeria*)

Alstroemeria needs shade, or semi-shade to light sun, and tolerates moderate frost. Collect seed or divide the clumps and separate the tubers.

Ranunculus

Ranunculus need a sunny position with good drainage. Plants grow easily from seed, though the best flowers come from the corms that grow from the first year's seedlings.

Snowdrop

Snowdrops need a cool position. They grow readily from seed as well as increasing bulbs. They also often reseed by themselves.

Watsonia

Watsonias are very tolerant. They grow from bulb increase or seed.

Some perennials

Bellis perennis

Bellis needs moist soil, and tolerates both frost and heat. Sow seed in spring or autumn or divide large clumps. Collect flowers that are past their prime, and keep them in a paper bag till the seed drops out.

Cactus

Needs vary according to the species of cacti. Seed can be collected after flowering or you can take cuttings. Cuttings should dry out before planting or they will rot; treat as for softwood cuttings.

Candytuft (*Iberis*)

Iberis needs full sun, good drainage and usually grows best in poor soils. Annuals grow from seed planted in spring; perennials should be planted from seed in autumn or old plants divided in autumn.

Christmas rose (*Helleborus*)

Christmas rose does best in cool to temperate climates with plenty or organic matter in the soil. They survive drought wonderfully. Collect ripe seed; this often sows itself. The varieties cross easily unless you protect them from cross-pollination, which can be great fun, as you'll end up with interesting variations. Large clumps can also be divided in autumn or spring.

Chrysanthemum

Chrysanthemums sucker. Dig them out in winter and divide up the clumps. They can also be grown from cuttings, which is useful if you want to take a small piece from a friend's garden.

Cuttings produce new, vigorous root systems and often have a better display of flowers than divided plants. Take cuttings, about 7 cm long, in spring, from the tips of stems. Remove the bottom leaves and plant the cutting up to halfway in sandy soil, or a mixture of half sand and half potting mix or peat.

Delphiniums

Delphiniums need a cool climate and are frost tolerant. They grow easily from seed collected as the flowers die down, but the seedlings won't come true-to-type. Crowns can be divided in early spring, just as they start to grow again, or cut the new shoots with a slight heel and treat them as softwood cuttings.

Dianthus

Dianthus needs full sun and a well-drained soil. Plants grow easily from seed, though seed is small and hard to collect. Put the dying flowers in a paper bag till the seed drops. Clumps can be divided after flowering, especially in winter, and cuttings can be taken at any time. A section of old stem kept moist in good, well-drained soil usually takes. This is best done in spring or autumn, or in cool, cloudy weather.

Gentians

Gentians need cool conditions, and do best in mountain areas. They grow easily from fresh seed, but hybridise readily. For the home gardener this is fun, rather than a problem. To get true-to-type plants, take cuttings or divide the roots in autumn or spring.

Geranium (*Pelargonium*)

Geraniums and pelargoniums are very hardy and tolerant, accepting moderate but not heavy frost. They are incredibly easy to grow from cuttings. Leave the cuttings in water at any time to root, or place them in a pot of soil, and within days new roots will form, as long as they aren't subjected to intense heat or cold. Seed often sets. Though seedlings may vary from their parents, this is a good way to increase your range of plants.

Gypsophila

This needs full sun. Annuals are grown from seed and perennials are usually grown from cuttings taken in spring.

Heath (*Erica*)

Needs vary according to the species of *Erica*, but most are usually extremely hardy. Seed can be collected after flowering, and should be planted on the top of the soil and covered with glass till it germinates. *Erica* seed must be sown fresh. Take cuttings of the new shoots that form after flowering and plant them in a mixture of peat and sand. Keep moist.

Hollyhock (*Alcea*)

Hollyhocks are both frost and drought hardy. Sow seed in spring or divide large plants with several spikes in autumn.

Divide hollyhock clumps with a spade

79

Marguerite daisy (*Chrysanthemum*)

Marguerite daisy needs full sun and tolerates only light frost. It grows easily from cuttings taken with some hardwood. This is best done in autumn, winter or spring.

Poppies (*Papaver* sp.)

Poppies need alkaline, well-drained, fertile soil. Annuals are grown from seed (they produce lots), and perennials from seed or root cuttings. Poppies can self-seed, too.

Verbena

Verbena needs full sun. Grow from seed or cuttings taken from prunings in autumn. Plant the cuttings directly in the garden. Large plants can also be divided.

Viola

Viola can be grown in full sun or partial shade, and needs a rich soil. It is easily grown from seed but may not come true-to-type. If you want to preserve a particular type, cut the plant down to ground level and take cuttings from the new shoots. Treat these like softwood cuttings.

Climbers

As a general rule, the more vigorous a plant, the easier it is to propagate. Climbers are generally very vigorous, and very easy to reproduce.

Bougainvillea

Bougainvilleas tolerate only mild frost, needing moist, deep soil and plenty of room. Take cuttings in summer and early autumn of new growth with a heel. Trim them back to about 60 cm, and plant as deeply as you can in sandy soil in semi-shade under an inverted jar (or in a glasshouse). Bottom heat improves the chances of success, but isn't necessary.

Carolina jasmine (*Gelsemium sempervirens*)

This is an evergreen, low-growing climber which likes a sunny position. Cuttings take during most of the year, though autumn cuttings usually strike best. Bottom heat is needed for cuttings in cold winters, or they may rot before spring. Take cuttings of lateral stems, with or without heels. Plant deeply and place in semi-shade.

Chilean bell-flower (*Lapageria rosea*)

Lapageria needs a cool climate, deep, moist soil, and semi-shade. Collect seed in late autumn. Keep it in the refrigerator and plant in spring. It should germinate in a couple of weeks.

Clematis

Take cuttings in late summer with at least three nodes. Keep them in the shade and under glass if possible, though they may take anyway.

Climbing fig

Take cuttings in late summer to early autumn, though cuttings will probably take at any time of the year. Remove all but the top four leaves, and plant up to the leaves. Keep in semi-shade and under glass if possible, though they usually take without this.

Honeysuckle (*Lonicera* sp.)

Honeysuckle is very tolerant of a wide range of conditions. Cut the stems into lengths, each with at least two nodes, in late autumn to early winter. Plant the lengths deeply. *Warning:* Do not grow near bushland! This one can be a menace.

Jasmine

Needs vary with species, but jasmines usually suit temperate climates. Cuttings can be taken at any time of the year, though autumn cuttings take best. Cut sections of the stems so that they have at least two nodes, and plant deeply. Cuttings should strike very easily. Some jasmines also sucker, and can become a pest. Some also set seed. GROW WITH CAUTION OR NOT AT ALL, AND NEVER NEAR BUSHLAND!

Mandevillea

Shelter mandevillea from strong winds and very heavy frost; otherwise it is very tolerant. Collect seed in late autumn and plant in spring. Most seed germinates in 1 to 2 weeks, and seedlings flower after 2 to 3 years.

Ornamental passionfruit

Needs vary according to species; some are frost-sensitive and some tolerate the cold. While cuttings take, beware of viruses. Seed is safer.

Take seed from ripe fruit, sow in spring, either separated from the pulp or fruit-and-all. The acid pulp helps the seed germinate more quickly. Dried seed can take a long time to germinate and may not be viable. If the fruit seems woody, don't use the seed — it may be virus-infected, though cold can also cause woody passionfruit. Dig out any infected plants.

Virginia creeper (*Parthenocissus quinquefolia*)

This is a deciduous, self-clinging climber which needs cold winters for best winter colour. It doesn't need support. Take cuttings in winter; these strike very easily. Take at least three nodes and bury two in moist, well-drained soil. I have also successfully taken cuttings in summer, keeping them in water till they rooted, then planting them out.

Wisteria

Wisteria is very strong-growing and needs a lot of room; it tolerates both frost and heat. *Warning:* Wisteria can strangle fences and lift off roofs. Grow it where it can't do any damage.

Collect seed in late autumn to early winter. Soak the seed in hot water for 3 days before sowing in early spring. Seedlings take about 4 years to flower.

Take stem cuttings in late spring from short laterals at the bottom of the vine. Keep moist, in semi-shade, and mist spray every day. Take root cuttings in late winter, about as long as your hand. Plant them so that they slope in a pot with the upper part of the root just poking out of the soil. Cover with an inverted jar and keep them moist in the semi-shade until they start to shoot in spring. Don't disturb them for the first year till feeder roots grow.

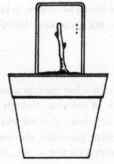

Cover wisteria cuttings with an inverted jar to keep them moist until they start to shoot in spring.

Shrubs and trees

Alder (*Alnus*)

Alders tolerate both cold and drought. Gather the seed in autumn; dry and store it over winter. Plant in spring, lightly covering the seed with soil, and leave in semi-shade. Seed may take some months to germinate. Don't transplant till well established. *Warning:* They can spread and become a pest.

Ash (*Fraxinus* sp.)

Ash is a cold-climate tree. Propagate by seed gathered in autumn or early winter when it is ripe. The flowering ash, *Fraxinus ornus*, will propagate from suckers.

Bamboo

Warning: Make sure the bamboo you have chosen is not an invasive one! Bamboos rarely seed. Divide clumps in spring or when the bamboo is sprouting (this can happen after rain rather than in spring), so that each clump has at least one new shoot. The outside growth, furthest from the centre, is usually the most vigorous.

Slice bamboo clumps with a spade.

Beech (*Fagus* sp.)

Beech is a cold-climate tree. Seed must be collected when ripe and stratified until sown in spring. Plants can also be grown from suckers.

Birch (*Betula* sp.)

Birch is a cool-climate tree, tolerating both frost and drought. Collect seed in autumn and sow at once in sandy soil. Don't cover the seed deeply, as it is fine and papery. Keep it moist, preferably covered with a glass jar in semi-shade or in a greenhouse.

Brooms (*Cytsus*)

Brooms are very tolerant. They grow easily from seed, but hybridise readily so may not grow true-to-type. Collect seed as soon as it is ripe in summer and sow it in sandy soil. Allow it to germinate in the shade, then move to semi-shade.

Cuttings can be taken in autumn, as long as your hand, with a heel. Place a little sand at the bottom of the hole before you plant them.

Warning: Many brooms are noxious weeds. Some supposedly sterile varieties may start to set seed after 15 years or more. Keep an eye on any broom, no matter who 'guaranteed' it was safe!

Buddleia

Buddleia is very tolerant and grows easily from seed. Take softwood cuttings in mid- to late summer, placing them in sandy soil in semi-shade. Hardwood cuttings can be taken from early to mid-winter and should be of the previous year's growth with a small heel. Place a little sand at the bottom of each hole in the garden and plant the cutting. Pinch out the top in spring as this encourages the plants to bush out.

Bunya (*Araucania bidwilli*)

Bunya needs an almost frost-free position in the open with a deep, moist, rich soil. But they'll grow happily in frosty gardens if they are sheltered by other trees. Propagation is by seed, cuttings from young branches (treat as hardwood cuttings) or basal suckers. Slice the suckers off with a sharp spade in autumn or spring.

Camellia

Sow camellia seed as soon as the pod slits. Sow in sandy soil in semi-shade and cover with an inverted jar (or place in a greenhouse).

Camellia japonica grows easily from cuttings. Take cuttings from the ends of branches, about as long as your hand, in late summer. A rooting powder will help them take, but isn't essential. Place the cuttings in sandy soil or a mix of one part sand to one part peatmoss. *Warning:* Tea camellias, with their single white flowers, produce lots of seedlings and may become a weed.

Cedar (*Cedrus* sp.)

Needs vary with species. Plants can be grown from seed, with germination taking up to 3 years.

Crab apple (*Malus* sp.)

Although the crab apple is a cold-climate tree, it will flourish in hot areas, though the fruit may not set. Propagation is by grafting onto seedlings. Cuttings may take but are very slow to grow.

Cypress (*Chamaecyparis* sp.)

Cypress tolerates a wide range of conditions. Although it will grow from seed, cuttings are preferable if you want an identical tree to the parent. Take cuttings in spring, or graft onto a seedling in spring.

Daphne

Daphne likes a temperate climate with a well-drained soil. It usually doesn't set seed, but if it does, plant it.

Daphne cuttings have a reputation for being hard to strike. Make sure they are taken in the middle of summer from new growth that can just be snapped rather than bent. They should be about 7.5 cm long and cut just below a node. Plant them as deep as you can in a mix of two parts sand to one of good soil or peatmoss. Water, and cover with an inverted jar. Don't let them dry out. They should start to root within 6 weeks.

Daphne can be layered in late winter, but don't cut the plant away for a year.

Dogwood (*Corms* sp.)

Dogwood species need full sun except for *Corms florida* which needs semi-shade. They tolerate both frost and heat, but don't colour well in the subtropics. Propagation is by seed, layering or hardwood cuttings in winter. Cuttings are slower, but retain the characteristics of the parent tree. Many dogwoods self-sow easily; the seed of the Japanese dogwood (*C. kousa*) doesn't germinate as easily as the others.

Elder (*Sambucus* sp.)

Elders tolerate both frost and heat. They grow from seed or hardwood cuttings; cool soils are best for the cuttings to take. If you need to take a cutting in mid-summer, try to strike it in water first on a windowsill, then pot it carefully when roots have formed. Plant out in late winter or early spring. *Warning:* These can become a weed.

Elm (*Ulmus*)

Elms like a cold climate but will survive in hot conditions. Propagation is generally be seed and sometimes by suckers, cuttings and layering.

Figs (*Ficus* sp.)

Some *Ficus* species need frost-free conditions; some tolerate light frost; and all need moisture, space and fertile soil. Use cuttings of young branches or layer woody branches – layering is best. Some figs sucker, and these suckers can be uprooted.

Fir (*Abies* sp.)

Fir grows in a cold climate and propagate by seed. Collect the cones in autumn and keep dry till the seed shakes out. Plant the seed in spring. Some firs will grow from a cutting, preferably with a heel. Hormone rooting powder is usually needed before they root.

Frangipani (*Plumeria rubra*)

Frangipani needs a frost-free, well-drained soil. Grow from cuttings of woody shoots. Make sure the latex is almost dry, then plant in sand that is only just wet. Cuttings are subject to rot easily, so keep them warm.

Fuchsia

Fuchsia needs a frost-free, semi-shaded position, or can be grown indoors. Take cuttings from the tips, about 5 to 7 cm long, from spring to mid-summer. Plant in sandy soil in semi-shade, preferably with an inverted glass cover, or in a shadehouse. Keep moist: a spray several times a day is best. They should root in 3 weeks.

Larger cuttings can be taken in winter. They strike readily, but are slower growing.

Gardenia

Take cuttings of new wood that can just be snapped. Cutting should be about as long as your hand, taken just below a node.

Hawthorn (*Crataegus oxyacantha*)

Hawthorn needs a cool to cold climate and tolerates heavy frost. Grow from seed which may take 2 to 3 years to germinate. *Warning:* In many areas hawthorns are a weed. Remove any that self-sow.

Hibiscus

Evergreen hibiscus tolerates only very mild frost, whereas deciduous hibiscus is frost-hardy. Take cuttings of evergreen hibiscus in spring from firm wood. The deciduous hibiscuses should be cut with a heel, in winter.

Holly (*Ilex aquifolium*)

Holly prefers a cold climate and tolerates heavy frost. It can be grown from seed or cuttings of partially-lignified shoots. For the cuttings to take, it needs good humidity and slightly acid soil.

Honey locust (*Gleditsia triacanthos*)

Honey locust tolerates frost, drought, poor soil and wind. It can be sown from seed, but this must be soaked for 36 hours before sowing. *Warning:* In many areas these are a weed. Remove any that self-sow.

Horse chestnut (*Aesculus hippocastanum*)

Horse chestnut needs deep, fertile soil, and tolerates frost. Seed must be planted before it is quite ripe. Seed won't germinate unless it is quite fresh. Pick the spiny fruit just as they start to fall from the tree.

Hydrangea

Take cuttings in winter, with a heel. Place some sand at the bottom of each hole and plant the cuttings in the garden in semi-shade. Keep them moist. Semi-mature cuttings can be taken in mid-summer. Cut off all but the top two leaves, and plant in sandy soil. Keep in the semi-shade.

Illawarra flame tree (*Brachychiton acerifolius*)

This tree needs a frost-free, well-drained, deep, moist soil. Propagate by seed or softwood cuttings under glass.

Jacaranda (*Jacaranda mimisifolia*)

The jacaranda needs a frost-free, deep, well-drained, moist soil. Propagate by seed or softwood cuttings.

Judas tree (*Cercis siliquastrum*)

This tree is hardy in many conditions, needing a well-drained soil. Grow from seed or root suckers. Plants flower at about 5 years old.

Juniper (*Juniperus* sp.)

Juniper tolerates frost. Use seed from cones that have been stratified for 18 months. Some varieties reproduce from cuttings taken in late summer. You only get juniper berries if there are male and female plants.

Laburnum (*Laburnum anagyroides*)

Laburnum is hardy in a wide range of conditions. Seed can be sown in autumn, or propagate by grafting onto seedlings or by suckers.

Larch (*Larix* sp.)

The larch is a cool-climate tree. Avoid exposed windy or coastal sites. Propagate by seed or softwood cuttings.

Lilac (*Syringa*)

Lilac needs a temperate climate. Propagation is best by layering in late winter. Use strong shoots from the previous year. *Warning:* Suckers may be a problem.

Linden (*Tilia* sp.)

Linden is a cold-climate tree which reproduces by seed, cuttings and sometimes suckers.

Magnolia (*Magnolia* sp.)

Magnolia is hardy in a wide range of climates, though prefers sunny positions and acid, well-drained soil. Grow from seed, layering or cuttings. Take softwood cuttings, about 10 cm long, in late winter and root in moist soil with a plastic bag over the pot.

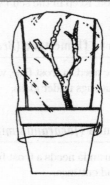

Cover softwood magnolia cuttings with a plastic bag to keep them moist.

Maidenhair tree (*Ginkgo biloba*)

Maidenhair tree tolerates mild frost and heat. Grow from seed or cuttings of softwood, or by grafting onto seedlings in order to avoid females that produce foul-smelling fruit.

Maple (*Acer* sp.)

Maples, including sugar maple (*Acer saccharum*), need cold winters for autumn colours. Grow from seed, though this may take some time to germinate and must be left undisturbed for several years. Use a fertile soil and place in semi-shade. Once the seedlings are well grown, transfer them to full sun; don't disturb the seedlings by repotting for 2 years. Graft onto the seedlings to retain the characteristics of the parent tree. *Warning:* In many areas these are a weed. Remove any that self-sow.

Mock orange (*Philadelphus*)

Mock orange tolerates both frost and heat. Winter is the best time for cuttings, but they will probably take at any time. Cuttings can be quite large, especially in winter, and can be planted straight into the ground.

Oak (*Quercus* sp.)

Oaks are generally cold-climate trees. They propagate from seed, which germinates best when just ripe. Don't store it. Plant seed as soon as it starts to drop. The holly oak (*Quercus lex*) suckers, and these can be planted.

Osage orange (*Maclura pomifera*)

This needs a deep, well-drained soil and tolerates frost, heat and drought, once established. Propagate by seed or root cuttings. Seed must be fresh from the fruit.

Palms

Most palms need frost-free conditions – this can be indoors. Palms are always grown from seed. This must be fresh, sometimes less than a week old. Place in sandy soil, one to a pot, and do not disturb the seedlings. Keep moist and warm.

Paulownia (*Paulownia* sp.)

Paulownias need deep, fertile soil. They tolerate both frost and heat, but grow fastest in subtropical conditions. They are usually grown from seed, though cuttings are possible. Both seedlings and cuttings grow very rapidly. Paulownias will often sucker.

Pepper tree (*Schinus molle*)

Pepper trees tolerate frost, heat and drought, as well as strong wind. They are grown from seed; the seedlings grow rapidly.

Photinia

Photinia is a very hardy, quick-growing plant. It tolerates drought, frost and heat. Take cuttings about 30 cm long, in late summer to early autumn, with a small heel. Cuttings should take in ordinary soil, but you can improve their chances by dusting with rooting powder. Water with a mister every day.

Pines (*Pines* sp.)

Needs vary with different *Pines* species. Grow from seed sown in spring, or from cuttings of young branches, taken with a heel, or terminal cuttings. *Warning.* In many areas these are a weed. Remove any that self-sow.

Pink silk tree (*Albizzia julibrissin*)

Albizzia tolerates both frost and heat. It grows easily from seed. Sow seed in spring after rubbing it for a few minutes with sandpaper. Soak it in warm water overnight to speed up germination.

Plane tree (*Platanus* sp.)

Platanus species are very hardy trees, tolerating heat, frost, smog and heavy pruning, but they need a deep soil. Seed is usually easy to germinate, or take cuttings of 2- or 3-year-old branchlets. *Warning.* In many areas these are a weed. Remove any that self-sow.

Poplar (*Populus* sp.)

Poplars need a cool climate for best colour, but otherwise are very tolerant. Propagate by seed or cuttings. The Lombardy poplar is almost always propagated by cuttings, as most trees in cultivation are male. Most poplar cuttings take easily. Use hardwood cuttings from autumn to spring – even cuttings several metres long will probably take. Plant in deep, moist soil. *Warning:* In many areas these are a weed. Remove any that self-sow.

Protea

Needs vary with species, but most proteas tolerate light frost and heat. Take cuttings in late summer to early autumn, about the size of your hand, from the top of strongly growing branches. Cut just below a bud. Keep moist and well-drained; mist with a spray every day. Some proteas take better than others. Proteas may also be grown from seed.

Prunus

The genus *Prunus* contains a large number of flowering and fruiting trees and shrubs. Most species are very tolerant. Collect seed from very ripe fruit. Remove the seed and keep it in the refrigerator until spring.

Cuttings from deciduous *Prunus* should be taken in winter, about 20 cm long. Place a little sand at the bottom of each planting hole. Cuttings from evergreen *Prunus* should be taken in late summer, about 10 cm long with a heel. A rooting powder increases the chances of success. Never let cuttings dry out.

Rhododendrons and azaleas

Needs vary according to species and variety; some are frost tender and others are hardy. Collect the seed pods when they start to turn brown. Sow the following spring, preferably on peatmoss or humus-rich soil. Keep moist and in semi-shade, especially after the seed has germinated. Seed won't come true-to-type as rhododendrons hybridise easily.

Most varieties will grow from cuttings in late summer or early autumn. Take tip growth, about 10 cm long, with or without a heel. Keep moist – preferably by spraying several times a day – and in semi-shade. They may take 3 months to root. *Warning:* In cool, wet areas these can become a weed. Remove any that self-sow.

Roses

The easiest way to grow roses is from cuttings. They will also grow from layering and seed.

Roses from seed

Roses don't breed true from seed, though you may get some interesting variations. Species roses (the old, wild ones) do grow true-to-type, but will take a long time to flower. Miniature roses, however, come reasonably true-to-type and can flower in the first year. Packets of rose seed are sometimes commercially available; otherwise take mature rose hips, chop them and soak until they ferment and the seed rises to the surface. Sow the seed in spring.

Layering

Any rose with long, low stems can be layered. Many ramblers layer themselves.

Cuttings

Most roses take very easily from cuttings. A mixture of half sand and half potting mix is best, though a friend does well with cuttings in pure sand, and the prunings which I just stick in the ground under the apple trees seem to take almost as well. Hybrid teas, especially yellow hybrid teas, are not supposed to form sturdy root systems from cuttings, but I have never found this a problem. Old-fashioned and rambling roses give almost 100 per cent success from cuttings, as do miniatures. The latter may flower in the first year.

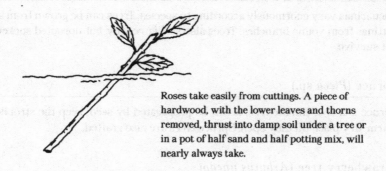

Roses take easily from cuttings. A piece of hardwood, with the lower leaves and thorns removed, thrust into damp soil under a tree or in a pot of half sand and half potting mix, will nearly always take.

Cuttings should be about as long as your hand, or as long as your finger for miniatures. Trim the cuttings to a leaf bud; remove the lower leaves and thorns, keeping at least two leaves or leaf buds. Dip in hormone powder if you wish. Bury two thirds of the cutting — just up to the first leaf. Keep the cuttings out of direct sunlight, and don't transplant them for at least a year.

Grafting and budding

Roses may be grafted onto the rootstock you have established by layering or cuttings. Most roses you buy will have been grafted or budded.

Breeding a new rose

This is fun, even if you don't get a show specimen. First, choose a seed parent and a pollen parent. Choose roses with characteristics you'd like to keep. Now choose a flower on your seed plant that is half open. Remove all the petals, pick off the anthers with a pair of tweezers, and wrap a paper bag over what's left of the flower.

The next day, cut a rose from the other parent, pull off the petals, brush the anthers against the stigma then put the paper bag back. Take the paper bag off after a fortnight. Wait for the hip to ripen in autumn; don't wait till it is shrivelled. Bury the hip in moist potting mix in a pot and leave out in the frost over winter. Bring the pot inside in early spring. Dig up the seed and squeeze it into a saucer of water. The seed that floats is infertile. Sow the seed that's sunk to the bottom.

Some of the plants will flower in the first year. Get rid of any spindly ones or those with poor flowers. You can either let the good ones grow or bud them onto other roses.

Russian olive (*Elaeagnus angustifolia*)

Russian olive tolerates cold and drought. It can be propagated by seed and hardwood cuttings. *Warning*: In many areas these are a weed. Remove any that self-sow.

She-oak (*Allocasuarina* sp.)

Casuarinas vary enormously according to species. Trees can be grown from seed or cuttings from young branches. Trees also sucker readily, but uprooted suckers may not survive.

Spruce (*Picea* sp.)

Spruce is a cool-climate tree. It can be propagated by seed; keep the strobiles in a warm, dry place till they open. Spruce trees are also grafted.

Strawberry tree (*Arbutus unedo*)

Arbutus tolerates frost and heat. Separate the seed from the fruit and dry it. Sow as soon as you can, covering lightly with soil. Keep moist, preferably with a glass jar or a plastic bag over the pot. Cuttings can be taken from mid- to late summer. Use semi-ripened wood of that year's growth, about as long as your hand. Place in sand and soil in semi-shade, and keep moist.

Verbena (*Aloysia triphylla*)

Verbena dies down in frost, but re-sprouts unless the ground is frozen. It tolerates drought. Take cuttings on new growth during mid-summer, with a heel of old wood. Place the cuttings in a mix of half soil and half sand; use bottom heat if possible. Cuttings start to root and sprout in 3 weeks. Hardwood cuttings are easier. Take them in winter, about 60 cm long. Protect them from frost till well-established.

Willow (*Salix* sp.)

Willows are very tolerant, but do need plenty of water and a deep soil. Willows will grow from seed, though cuttings are usually used. Quite large branches can be planted in moist soil; most will take and become an instant large tree. Many weeping willows are hybrids and may not come true-to-type from seed. Take cuttings from the female trees – the ones producing the seed. (Seeds have long, silky hairs that help them spread.) Willows also reproduce naturally when twigs are broken off in a flood and root in river bends, or as the old trees break down and the fallen branches take root. *Warning:* In many areas most willow species are a weed. Check with your local Department of Agriculture.

6 Native plants

Sometimes it seems a misnomer to call all Australian plants 'native'. Native to where, exactly?

Australia is a large country; a garden can have red-flowering gums from Western Australia, a grevillea from Victoria and a waratah from New South Wales, and still be called native.

The plants that grow best in your area will probably be plants that are true natives of that area — ones that evolved there and have adapted to its conditions. Even trees and shrubs that grow naturally in your area but have been raised elsewhere may not be as suited to your conditions as ones you raise from seed collected in the area.

It is illegal to take seeds and cuttings from reserves or national parks. It also reduces those plants' chances of propagating themselves naturally. Stick to cuttings from gardens or privately-owned bushland, with permission of the owner. If you particularly want rare stock from a national park or reserve, approach the local ranger for permission first. It is illegal to collect some seeds even on private land. If you are collecting large numbers, it is best to check with your state's national parks service, forestry department or the state herbarium.

Seed

I find great satisfaction in growing native plants from seed I've collected myself from the natural vegetation on my land — without the interference of seed companies and without money changing hands.

Warning: Native plants can be weeds too! Pittosporums, many grevilleas, wattles, erigeron and others can spread into areas where they don't naturally grow, choking out the native plants. ALWAYS keep a look out for ANY plant that spreads or grows too successfully!

Collecting the best seed

All seed, native or not, should be from the best plant you can find. The larger the seed, the better. Avoid pest-prone trees, spindly trees, or trees with problems, unless other plants are not available.

Try not to collect seed from isolated trees, as is may not all be pollinated, and often self-pollinated seed isn't as good as that pollinated by other trees. Collect seed from several trees or shrubs if you can, not just one, for more genetic diversity and as a safeguard in case some are infertile.

Methods used to collect seed are, to:

* lay a tarpaulin under the plant and check it every week;
* tie an old stocking over the seed head so the seed is caught as it falls;
* use a long stick with a knife on one end to cut off seed heads. You can nail an old can under the knife to catch the seeds if necessary;
* attach a rake to a long stick and rake down seeds;
* use a long stick to knock down ripe seeds (but don't damage the tree);
* climb the tree (you can also use an abseiling harness);
* use bows and arrows with string attached to pull down the tops of high seed-bearing branches;
* shoot down high twigs with a rifle (if you have a permit).

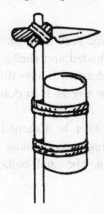

A simple seed collector for tall trees can be made from a knife fastened on a stick above a collecting pot or old tin can.

Storing seed

Once you have your seed, dry it as soon as you can. Don't store green seed — it will rot, cook, or may even germinate prematurely.

Dry the seeds on a sheet or rack in the sun. If the fruit is very fleshy, cut it away first or let it ferment till the flesh can be rubbed away. A little dried fruit attached to the seed seems to help the seed germinate later, even if it isn't so good for keeping.

Some rainforest seed, especially fruit seed, shouldn't be dried or stored. Sow it straightaway.

Unlike vegetable seed, glass jars with screw-top lids are excellent for most native seed. Make sure both jar and seed are as dry as possible. Keep in a cool, dark place. Don't let the temperature rise above 25°C. Label your seed. Seed can last longer than your memory.

Identifying seed

If in doubt about which plant you have, send some to your state herbarium. Say where the plant is found, when it flowered or set seed, what it looked like, and any other information you have, as well as specimens of leaves, fruit, flowers or seed.

Mutations

Mutations are natural variations in plants. In the past 20 years of wandering round the bush, I've found several natural variations in natives, such as a green wonga vine and a pale purple clematis. Some of these are a lot more striking than the parent. If you want to propagate natural variations, you need to take cuttings, as the seed will almost certainly be crossed with surrounding plants that may not have the characteristics you want.

Seedlings

Many native plants reseed themselves readily. Any area that is regularly dug, covered in moist mulch or otherwise shaded and sheltered, will be a likely spot for seedlings. Many of the young plants will have different leaves from the adults and may be taken at first for weeds. If in doubt, pot a few seedlings and wait till they grow larger.

Seeds with thick or waxy coats should either be softened by covering with boiling water and leaving to soak overnight, by rubbing with sandpaper, or by using a needle to prick the strophiole (the small bulbous bit on the seed near the stalk).

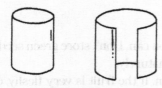
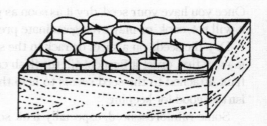

Make tubes for your native plants by taking the tops and bottoms off tin cans, slitting them, and packing them in a box.

Hybrids

Many of our native plants naturally grow in a very small area. Once taken out of this area and grown with other plants of the same species, many natives readily cross. Where we live, the red- and yellow-flowered boxes cross frequently; and many eucalypts, callistemons, some acacias, and leptospermums will also cross.

Remember that when you take seed from around the garden you may not get offspring that are true-to-type. This will almost certainly be the case if you take seed from any of the modern native hybrids. On the other hand, like many seedlings, if you are only breeding for your own pleasure or garden, or for gifts, this may not matter. The variety may be fun, and if you prune out the less hardy specimens, you may end up with a more attractive plant or one more suited to your area.

It's also worth remembering, if you live near the bush, that some of your garden plants may hybridise with bush plants — possibly causing, without intending to, some of those plants to become extinct, as hybrid seedlings take over from the original plants.

Cuttings

Follow the basic techniques in taking all cuttings (see Chapter 2). If possible, take cuttings from the top of the plant when it is actively growing and not flowering. Along the coast, this is most likely to be in spring and summer, or in autumn or early winter (when the rains have started) in inland areas. Don't take cuttings in dry times, as they are less likely to root.

Remember that the growth points are at the nodes (around the leaves on the stem). You need to have at least one node below the ground and one above ground. Make sure all below-ground leaves are taken off before you put the cutting in the ground, otherwise they may rot and the rot may spread to the cutting.

Cuttings of fern-leaf grevilleas strike best in late summer; many other hybrid grevilleas only strike at particular times of the year. If you fail at one time, try another. Remember that new wood takes faster in warm weather, and old wood is better in cold conditions. Some plants, however, take better from either old or new wood. The following take best from new growth after flowering: *Telopea, Callistemon, Grevillea*, some *Melaleuca* species, *Boronia* and *Thryptomene saxicola. Prostanthera, Olearia, Verticordia*, some *Melaleuca* species and *Thrypotmene* take best from new growth with a bit of old growth.

Keeping cuttings

Cuttings lose water from the moment they are picked, so wrap them in wet newspaper and place them in a plastic bag. Open the bag at night and re-water them, then leave the bag open till the morning. If possible, put the cuttings in a refrigerator or an esky. Most cuttings will stay viable for about 3 weeks if treated properly. Plant as soon as you can.

Keep cuttings moist by wrapping them in damp newspaper and keeping them in a plastic bag until you can plant them.

Softwood cuttings

Prostanthera (mint bush), *Helichrysum* (everlastings), *Olearia* (daisy bush), *Pimelea*, *Isopogon* (drumsticks), *Melaleuca* (paperbark), *Verticordia*, *Chamelaucium* (Geraldton wax flower), *Correa*, *Boronia*, *Eriostermon* and *Grevillea* all grow well from softwood cuttings.

Snip off a piece of the top new growth in late spring or summer, about as long as your thumb (except for Correa which should be about the length of your hand). Take off all but two leaves. Cut off any stem below the first node, as it may rot below ground. Plant the cutting firmly at an angle with at least two nodes in the soil, and stake it. If the cutting rocks, the plant will lose contact with the soil, and roots won't form.

Hardwood cuttings

These are made from last year's growth that has turned from green to grey or brown. Woody cuttings take longer to grow than softwood cuttings, but many native plants will only take from woody cuttings. Waratahs, *Brachysema lanceoiatum* (Swan river pea-bush), some grevilleas and some eucalypts grow best from woody cuttings.

Make sure the cutting is smooth, with no rough edges. This is often even more important with natives than other plants as they can have a greater tendency to rot. The soil needs to be mostly sand. Some people prefer to add one part of soil from where the plant is growing to the sand, as the natural organisms around the plant are sometimes necessary for the new cuttings to grow well. If you fail at your first attempt to take cuttings, you may like to try this, or you may like to use hormone powders for cuttings that take a long while to root.

Grafting

Many natives can be grafted. Unlike most imported plants, however, there is no 'best time' to graft natives in Australia. Most natives grow best after rain, but this will vary from place to place. Try to graft at the beginning of your rainy season, or when you notice that most of your native plants are producing new growth. Plants that are actively growing are more likely to take when grafted.

Budding

Again, most natives can be budded, which is a good way to get different flowers on the same bush, or a more attractive plant on a hardy rootstock. On the other hand, large buds are mostly found in plants with very cold winters, and the buds of many natives are small, and hard to handle unless you are an expert.

Take the buds in autumn, as it may be hard to find dormant buds at most times of the year.

Some popular natives

Acacia (wattle)

Sow seed in spring, first rubbing it with sandpaper for a few minutes to scratch the hard coating. Wattle seed can also be heated in a non-oiled frying pan until a couple of seeds burst — plant the rest. Soaking in warm water overnight speeds up the germination. You need to wait about 3 weeks for seed to germinate.

Heat wattle seeds in a dry frying pan until a couple burst; then plant the rest.

Angophora

Cover seed with paper or hessian till it germinates. This should take a couple of weeks. Don't let it dry out or become waterlogged. Water with chamomile tea to prevent damping off.

Anigozanthus (kangaroo-paw)

This plant tolerates heat, mild frost and drought. Collect seeds after flowering and sow in sandy soil during warm weather. Clumps can also be divided, but don't make them too small or they may take a long while to flower or grow again.

Baeckea

Take tip cuttings of half-ripened wood, about 10 cm long with a small heel, in mid- to late summer, depending on the growth of the plant. Plant in sandy soil and cover with an inverted glass jar.

Banksia

Most banksia cones have to be heated to release the seed. Leave them in the oven at 120°C for an hour or till the seed is ejected. Plant in pots and cover with glass or plastic until the seed germinates. Try not to disturb the roots of the young seedlings. Some banksias are easily propagated by cuttings; others rarely take. Use tip cuttings of last year's growth, about 10 cm long with a heel, in mid- to late summer. Place in sandy soil or potting mix and cover with an inverted glass jar, or place in a cold frame.

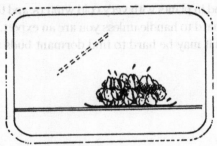

Leave banksia cones in the oven at 120°C until the seeds are ejected.

Boronia

Boronias need a well-drained soil. Seeds germinate best at about 15°C. Cover with an inverted glass jar, and don't let the seedlings dry out. Take cuttings in late summer to autumn, about 5 cm long, from half-ripe tip growth or woody laterals with a heel. Use sandy soil with a layer of sand on top. Cover the cuttings with glass or plastic and keep cool in the semi-shade. The temperature should not rise above 17°C.

Callistemon (bottlebrush)

Callistemon grows easily from seed. Leave the seed capsules in a warm place to open. Sow the seed in sandy soil. Cuttings can be taken in mid- to late summer from half-ripe terminal shoots, about 10 cm long. Place in sandy soil, and use a cold frame if possible.

Casuarina

Needs vary enormously according to species. Place the ripe cones in a paper bag to catch the fine seed.

Clematis aristata (Australian clematis)

Clematis tolerate moderate frost and heat. Collect seed in late summer and sow in spring. Cuttings should be taken in spring. Make sure that there is a leaf node with two leaves on it at both the top and bottom of the cuttings. Remove one leaf and leave the other. Place in sandy soil and cover with an inverted glass jar.

Eucalyptus

Eucalypts have varying needs according to species. Collect seed about 6 months after flowering. Some species take from cuttings, but this is a matter for experimentation.

Grevillea

Grevilleas are generally hardy plants, tolerant of a wide range of conditions. Specific needs will vary with species. To collect seed place a paper bag over the green capsules. Seed is quickly dropped when the capsules turn brown. Seed is often scarce and may not germinate well.

Hakea

Hakeas like hot dry summers, and tolerate coastal conditions. Wait 2 months after sowing for seed to germinate.

Hardenbergia

Hardenbergia needs full sun or semi-shade. It will tolerate light frost. Plants grow easily from seed. Wait till the capsules turn black and break open naturally.

Helichrysum

Helichrysum tolerates frost, heat and drought. Collect dry flowers and scatter them, leaves and all, in spring.

Leptospermum (tea-tree)

Collect the seed as soon as the capsules ripen. The seed is very fine and may have to be collected in a paper bag placed over the ripening fruit. Most cultivated leptospermums are hybrids and won't come true-to-type.

Take cuttings in late summer or autumn. Take short lateral growth with a heel, about 5 cm long, and plant the cuttings in sandy soil under a glass jar (or use a cold frame).

Melaleuca (paperbark, honey-myrtle)

Sow melaleuca seeds in spring. Cuttings can be taken in mid-summer from semi-ripe side or terminal shoots, with a slight heel.

Prostanthera (mint bush)

Prostanthera is frost and heat tolerant. Take half-matured tip growth cuttings in mid-summer, and plant them in semi-shade or in a glasshouse.

Telopea (waratahs)

Sow seed in spring, one to a pot as seedlings can easily be killed if the roots are disturbed when transplanting. Use a sandy soil. Seedlings are prone to damping off. Keep in an airy, non-humid spot.

Thryptomene

Thryptomene is frost and heat hardy. Rub the seed with sand before sowing, and be prepared to wait a year. Take cuttings of side shoots in mid-summer; plant in a mix of five parts sand to one part compost or peatmoss. Keep moist under a glass jar or in a cold frame.

7 Herbs

Like most plants, herbs were once wild, growing and propagating themselves. Herbs, however, also have a long history of cultivation. Like all plants that have been popularly grown for a long time, herbs are easily grown from a piece thrust into a pocket, or a few seeds wrapped in a handkerchief.

Most herbs are hardy as long as they have their preferred conditions: like dry sun for lavender, moist semi-shade for woodruff, and deep, rich soil for valerian.

Cuttings

Most herbs that 'snap' (produce old wood) can be reproduced by cuttings. Take cuttings from autumn (in mild areas) through to spring. Spring sowing is best in cold areas, as the cutting may rot in very cold weather. The cutting can be simply a snip off a low branch, and may have a 'heel' — a piece of the stem. Cuttings with a heel strike more readily, but herbs usually strike very easily anyway. If you have moist ground, you will rarely have any failures.

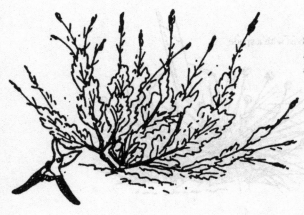

Snip off herb cuttings as near to the ground as you can.

My herb cuttings are simply prunings thrust into the ground wherever I want them.

Herbs that reproduce from cuttings include:

- artemisia (wormwood)
- basil
- bay tree
- box
- geranium
- hyssop
- lavender
- mint
- rosemary
- rue
- sage
- thyme
- verbena (lemon or lime)
- winter savory

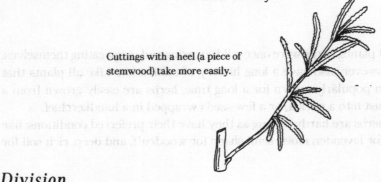

Cuttings with a heel (a piece of stemwood) take more easily.

Division

Mints, rue, chives and other plants that form large spreading roots can be divided. This is best done in cool weather, but can usually be done at any time.

Dividing clumps needs a bit more care, and should probably be done in winter to minimise moisture loss. Clumps should be divided when the centre starts looking a bit thin, or the clump becomes too bulky. Lift the whole plant out of the soil and pull it apart, or, if necessary, slice it with a sharp spade. Replant the pieces in new ground as deeply as they were before.

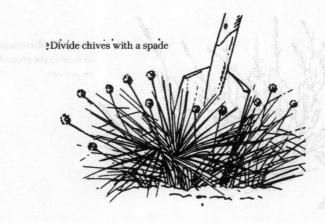

Divide chives with a spade

Herbs that reproduce by division include:

- bergamot
- catmint
- chives
- comfrey
- lemon balm
- lime balm

- lovage
- marjoram
- all mints
- oregano
- tarragon — French and Russian
- thyme

Seed

Most herbs can be grown from seed. This is best sown in spring to mid-summer. Some herbs should be sown as soon as the seed ripens, angelica is the most crucial of these, as seed will deteriorate in about 10 days (which is why bought angelica seed rarely germinates). Others in the same category are chervil, cowslips and woad. Once you have these plants, however, they will probably reseed themselves. Their short length of fertility is made up for by their vigorous germination. Most herb seed, though, lasts for at least 2 years.

Parsley seed is very slow to germinate. Pour boiling water over it, leave overnight, then plant it.

Herbs which grow from seed include:

- angelica
- basil
- borage
- chervil
- dill
- fennel (a weed in most areas; especially bronze fennel)
- feverfew (a weed in most areas)
- ginseng
- horehound (a weed in most areas)
- lemon balm (may become a weed)
- lime balm
- marjoram (a weed in moist areas)
- mint
- oregano
- parsley (curled, Italian, turnip rooted)
- purslane
- sorrel
- summer savory
- woad
- wormwood (can become a weed in harsh, sunny areas)

Cross-pollination

Many herbs cross-pollinate with other varieties. For example, different lavenders may cross, though lavender won't cross with any other herb. In practice, this may not matter in the home garden, where you may only have one variety growing anyway. Parsley cross-pollinates, but I have three varieties growing and so far they have bred true-to-type, as have my basils, in spite of the range I have growing.

The only conspicuous new varieties I have produced have been from lavender crossings, mint crossings and a marjoram-oregano cross — which is delicious, drought and frost hardy, and even outgrows kikuyu. Lavender is more easily grown from a cutting than seed, though the seeds grow easily, and crossings are often interesting.

If you want to save seed for sale or to preserve an interesting line, use the paper bag or nylon stocking methods from the chapter on vegetable seed, and pollinate the plants yourself. I find the best way to collect herb seed is in old nylon stockings. Tie them around a bush as soon as it stops flowering, before the seed starts to ripen, and remove them a couple of months later. Many herbs will produce seedlings around themselves if the soil is bare and moist. Tuck a little potting mix around the base as the seed starts to fall.

Collect herb seed by wrapping the seed head in an old nylon stocking.

Layering

Layering is a good method for getting new plants from old woody ones. Pin the bottom branch of your old sage bush to the ground and cover it with a little soil, leaving the top of the bush poking out. You can do the same with basil bushes as soon as they are big enough. The bottom basil branches may not be long enough to reach the soil, so add more soil around the base of the plant till you can cover part of it.

Layering is useful for obtaining new plants of basil, bay tree, mint and sage.

8 Indoor Plants

Most house plants are very easily propagated by the amateur; in fact, you could say that they became house plants because they are so easily propagated. They respond to much the same propagation techniques as other plants — by cutting, layering and division.

Indoor plants can be grown in plastic pots, clay pots, old teapots, mugs, on saucers, or in any container as long as it has a hole in the bottom for drainage. Old ginger jars or wine flagons are excellent for rooting cuttings in water. Clay pots are porous; they let excess water out and air in so that the soil can breathe, but this does mean that you have to water more often. Clay pots can also harbour disease, so wash them well, then soak in vinegar and water before replanting.

Plastic pots are thin and the soil inside them heats up and cools down quickly. If possible, don't leave them on windowsills and other exposed places.

Remember that plants in pots are more exposed than plants in the garden. Extremes of either heat or cold can have a fast and fatal effect.

If roots start to grow through the bottom of a pot, the plant probably needs dividing and repotting.

Seed

Many house plants set seed, but the seed may not be fertile — there are few bees, wasps, breezes or other pollinating devices indoors to do the job. If you want to collect seed from your indoor plants, try using a very fine paint brush to transfer pollen to the stigmas (the same as for hand-pollinating vegetables).

Many tropical plants can be grown from seed and kept as indoor plants, even in cold areas. I have heard of hand-pollinated avocados fruiting in centrally-heated Canadian houses. Try growing bananas indoors (there are ornamental bananas that grow from seed), or coffee bushes, passionfruit or pepper vines.

Plants in water

This is the easiest way to propagate house plants, and can be used for a surprising number of them.

Fill a clean bottle with clean water and cover the top with aluminium foil, sealing it with a rubber band. Poke the cutting through the foil till the stem is in the water and a leaf rests on the foil. Try African violets, ivies, busy lizzies, spider plants and sweet potato. Experiment with other plants. You can also just try rooting the cutting in a container of water.

Make sure the water is kept topped up, and replace it if algae start to grow. Most cuttings need no other feeding, though a liquid fertiliser can be used if the old leaves start to yellow, or a few drops of fresh urine may be added every few weeks.

Plantlets

Many indoor plants, like spider plants or mother of thousands, produce tiny complete plants on the ends of their runners. Peg these down in another pot with a couple of toothpicks, still leaving them attached to their parent.

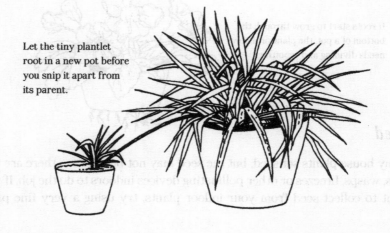

Let the tiny plantlet root in a new pot before you snip it apart from its parent.

You can even let them root in the same pot as the parent, using an old match-box or something similar which can then be lifted out and planted, box and all, well-soaked. Don't use the standard cutting mix of peat or soil and sand for this, as the small plantlets need more food because they are still growing strongly. Use sterilised garden soil or normal potting mix (or even normal garden soil), as long as it's fertile.

Root clumps

Potted plants that form large clumps can be divided. This is the classic way of propagating the Victorian parlour favourite, the aspidistra. Water the plant well, take it out of its pot, shake off as much soil as you can, then tease the roots apart. Some tough roots may need slicing with a sharp knife. Pot the clumps as soon as you can in fresh potting mix or new soil.

Cuttings

Most indoor plants are tropical or semi-tropical; otherwise they wouldn't thrive in the winter warmth of houses. Cuttings usually need a minimum temperature of about 18°C to start to root. Try to keep the temperature as even as possible — not warm during the day when you have the heater on, and cold when you go to bed.

Most house plants will provide viable cuttings at any time of the year — there are few seasonal differences inside. Late spring and early summer are probably best though, so that cuttings have a whole growing season to establish before winter. If your indoor plants have wood that will snap, treat the cuttings like hardwood cuttings.

With indoor cuttings, surrounding the pots with plastic wrap not only stops the cuttings from drying out, but it is also less messy.

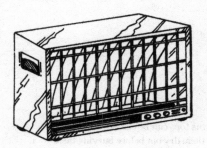

Try not to let house plants toast by the heater, then freeze when you go to bed.

Some easy indoor plants

African violets

Everyone, at some time, gets given an African violet. As soon as they stop flowering (or even while they are flowering), pick off a leaf and jab it in potting mix. Each leaf should grow. As African violets don't like humidity, don't cover the leaf cuttings with plastic. Neglect grows better plants than too much care.

African violet leaves can also be grown in water.

Insert an African violet leaf into the soil; then wait for it to grow new roots and more leaves.

Bromeliads

Bromeliads form clumps, so cut off the offsets or smaller clumps. Repot these as soon as you can.

Cactus

Cacti need a good potting mix covered with a layer of clean sand, with another layer (if possible) of small stones as mulch.

Cut off the top bulbous part of a cactus. This can either be planted shallowly as it is, or the outside bottom edge can be peeled back, much as you would peel an orange. This means that the roots grow from the stronger core.

Let the cuttings dry out before you plant them — at least overnight. They should be planted just below the pebbly top, in the sand, so that the roots can grow down in the soil. if the cuttings are small or spindly, stake them to stop them from falling over in the loose sand.

Cactus tops can be cut and rooted. Let them dry out before burying them shallowly.

Cumquats

These make excellent indoor plants. Plant a seed, wait for the seedling, then transplant. Keep in a sunny spot near a window.

Ferns

Ferns grow from spores. To collect seed, look for the dark brown specks under a leaf (they should be dark brown, not light brown), and put them in a paper bag. Keep the seed in the bag for a couple of days, then shake the bag well. The spores should shake to the bottom of the bag.

Fill a clay pot with a mixture of potting mix and sand, about half and half, with a little charcoal added to keep the mixture sweet. Alternatively, use a combination of half peat and half garden soil with a little sand and charcoal. Moisten the mix and press it down firmly, then shake on the spores. Cover with a sheet of glass (I have used a glass plate for this or the top of a photo frame), and put the pot in a bucket of water so that only the bottom of the pot is covered. Make sure there isn't too much water or the pot might tip over. The pot needs to be clay, not plastic, so that the water can permeate through the sides as well as the bottom.

Never let the pot dry out, get cold or be in direct sunlight. After about 6 weeks to 4 months, a mossy sort of growth will appear. This will soon start to produce miniature ferns. As soon as you can recognise a classic fern leaf shape, take the glass off. Pot the plants as soon as they are large enough to handle.

Ferns can also be grown by division. Many ferns have rhizomes (roots) that spread out, so that smaller clumps appear to one side. Wet the whole pot, empty it, loosen the soil and cut through the rhizome. Repot as soon as you can, preferably in a mixture of one part soil, one part sand, and four parts peatmoss. Don't use ordinary commercial potting mix as it may have too much fertiliser dissolved in it and this can kill the fern. You can even use garden soil with a little added sand or, better still, a mix of half compost and half sand.

Gasteria (and other succulents)

Pull off a long leaf, cut it into sections and plant each section in sandy soil. For succulents with smaller fleshy leaves, it's better to plant the whole leaf, as a small section may not have enough stored nutrients to keep it growing long enough to root.

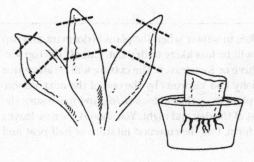

Succulent cuttings should be left to dry, then planted in sand. Each section of the plant will grow new roots.

Golden pothos (*rhaphidophora aurea*)

Take cuttings in spring and summer and treat as softwood cuttings. Make sure at least one leaf is buried.

Indoor figs

Figs can be air layered like the rubber plants, or long branches can be fixed with a few toothpicks in a new pot of soil. Cut the branch on the bottom side, cover the end with potting mixture and wait for roots to form.

Monstera deliciosa

Air layered cuttings can be taken from the top of monsteras, but unlike the rubber plant, the parent plant looks peculiar afterwards as the top doesn't become bushy again. They are better grown from seed, though the seed may not germinate unless the temperature is at least 30°C.

Orchids (*cymbidium*)

Divide orchids as soon as the flowers have died. Cut away the flower spikes, shake off the soil, and try to separate the plants. These may naturally divide into two or more clumps, but if not, use a sharp knife. Cut away old, shrivelled roots, leaving the new white ones. Each new plant should have at least half a dozen new roots. Firm down compost around the roots and keep the new plants in a humid, semi-shaded spot, say at the bottom of a bush house.

Poinsettias

Poinsettias are temperamental and need to be kept moist. Take a cutting just below a leaf. Remove the leaf and let the cutting dry. Stick the cutting into pure peatmoss or compost, and cover the pot with plastic wrap. Spray the cutting at least twice a day with a mister and keep it out of strong sunlight. As soon as the cutting is growing well, take off the leafy tips so that the plant bushes out; otherwise you'll have a long, thin straggler.

Rubber plant

Rubber plant cuttings should be taken in winter when the plant is dormant and sap isn't flowing as freely, so the plant will be less likely to dry out. Cut off the top section of the old plant, with the top three or four leaves. The cutting will be attractive right from the start, and will be bushy and vigorous by the end of the next season. Let the cutting dry out before you plant it, so that it doesn't rot, and make sure the temperature is at least 21°C for most of the day and night. You should see new leaves in about a month as the new roots form. Use the common mixture of half peat and half sand.

Cuttings can also be taken of a lower leaf with a bit of stem. These also take easily, but look peculiar. It can be a year or more before they have an attractive shape. Taking the top of a rubber plant also encourages it to bush out, and is a good way of pruning spindly bushes.

Rubber plants can be air layered. Take a leaf off where you want the roots to form and make a notch in the stem; it should be about half as thick as the stem and as long as your little finger. Dust with rooting powder, though this isn't essential, then wrap the lot in spagnum moss and a plastic bag tied with string. You should be able to see the roots grow through the clear plastic. If no roots form in 2 to 4 months, try again. When there is a nice handful of roots, cut off the new plant just below the roots and plant it. Make sure the temperature stays around at least 21°C and keep the new plant fairly dry until it is well-established.

Sweet potato vine

Three-quarter fill a jar with water and rest a sweet potato on two toothpicks jammed a third of the way up the jar. It is best to choose a potato that already shows some shoots as many have been treated to stop shoots from appearing. Avoid strong sunlight, like a window ledge. If you want very fast growth, place the jar in a dark cupboard for a fortnight. Otherwise, place it on a table and watch it sprawl. Keep the water level even and the plant should become enormous in a couple of years.

Index